Froth on the Cappuccino

Froth on the *Cappuccino*

How Small Pleasures
Can Save Your Life

Maeve Haran

HAY HOUSE

Australia • Canada • Hong Kong
South Africa • United Kingdom • United States

First published and distributed in the United Kingdom by:
Hay House UK Ltd, 292B Kensal Rd, London W10 5BE.
Tel.: (44) 20 8962 1230; Fax: (44) 20 8962 1239. www.hayhouse.co.uk

Published and distributed in the United States of America by:
Hay House, Inc., PO Box 5100, Carlsbad, CA 92018-5100. Tel.: (1) 760 431
7695 or (800) 654 5126; Fax: (1) 760 431 6948 or (800) 650 5115.
www.hayhouse.com

Published and distributed in Australia by:
Hay House Australia Ltd, 18/36 Ralph St, Alexandria NSW 2015. Tel.: (61) 2
9669 4299; Fax: (61) 2 9669 4144. www.hayhouse.com.au

Published and distributed in the Republic of South Africa by:
Hay House SA (Pty), Ltd, PO Box 990, Witkoppen 2068. Tel./Fax: (27) 11 467
8904. www.hayhouse.co.za

Published and distributed in India by:
Hay House Publishers India, Muskaan Complex, Plot No.3, B-2, Vasant Kunj,
New Delhi – 110 070. Tel.: (91) 11 41761620; Fax: (91) 11 41761630.
www.hayhouse.co.in

Distributed in Canada by:
Raincoast, 9050 Shaughnessy St, Vancouver, BC V6P 6E5. Tel.: (1) 604 323
7100; Fax: (1) 604 323 2600

A catalogue record for this book is available from the British Library.

ISBN 978-1-4019-1105-8

Printed and bound in Europe for Imago.

Dedication

For my mother, Mollie Haran, full-time doctor and mother of four, whose own small pleasure was to lock the bathroom door and retreat into the tub with a glass of sherry and the novels of Georgette Heyer.

At least I know where I got it from.

To my family, the bedrock of everything, and my friends (some of whom have supplied their own pleasures, thank you).

Introduction

We live in a world where change is fast and we can't control it. Life is stressful and sometimes we feel powerless. We may not have religious faith to depend on. Families, once round the corner, are often either fractured or distant. Even marriage isn't the reliable safety net against loneliness it once was. We are richer than ever before and we buy more goods than any previous generation, and yet statistics keep showing that we're unhappier than ever.

So what can you rely on that isn't immoral, illegal or (too) fattening to make you feel that, despite all this, life is wonderful?

The answer is small pleasures.

Lady Thatcher, when asked what gave her greatest satisfaction in life, replied, 'Taking the fluff out of the tumble-dryer.' I know exactly what she meant. Some tiny tasks do provide an inordinate amount of pleasure and satisfaction. Even changing a fuse or tidying a cupboard can restore a feeling of being in control.

Part of the answer to the problems of modern life lies in re-establishing connectedness. Holding the hand of a small child connects you to future generations. Talking to shopkeepers instead of always using an anonymous supermarket connects you to your area. Enjoying the sight of mist on a cornfield connects you to nature. Folding sheets and towels can connect you to the past, perhaps to a memory of your mother. Recycling connects you to the future of the planet. Having a glass of champagne in the bath connects you to sensual pleasure!

One irony is that modern gurus recommend we pare down and declutter our lives, throwing away anything we don't continually use. This even goes as far as chucking out old friends if they are dull or boring or of no use to us. And yet this clutter, both of things and people, is the very stuff of life, often coloured by our history and glowing with emotional significance, and we throw it away at our peril.

Small pleasures are nothing new. When Adam delved and Eve span, Eve probably looked up and said, 'Wow, Adam, look at that fantastic sunset!' Being a man, he was probably too focused on mowing the Eden lawn in straight lines to notice.

When I was doing some research for a book on the

seventeenth century I came across a wonderful entry from the diary of Mary Rich, Countess of Warwick. This observant lady commented on the pleasure of 'walking in autumn among dead leaves', 'upon seeing a silk-worm spin' and – my personal favourite – 'upon seeing a hen of my lady Essex Rich which ever laid her eggs inside the house'. And that was in the year 1651!

For centuries small pleasures have lifted women from the drudgery of housework, the exhaustion of family life, the grief of loss and the loneliness of old age. Our modern pleasures – the ones that lift and cheer us – may be different, but they still have the same effect. In fact, being part of that long continuum of female enjoyment of small things is a pleasure in itself.

Men, too, draw enormous sustenance from everyday enjoyments: chopping wood, fixing things, drinking good beer, putting their CD collections in the right order!

The wonderful truth is that we're surrounded by small miracles and delicious delights and we just need to open our arms and embrace them.

Listing Three Good Things

We all have an inner voice that criticizes us and undermines us. Often it encourages us to compare our lives with other people's and feel envious. Other people seem to have better lives, newer cars, more money, nicer children. Or even, in a subtler way, they may seem to get what they want more, or be calmer or more sorted than we feel ourselves.

The answer, when the envy demon gets his poison claws into you, is to remind yourself that envy only damages one person: you. Instead of feeling envious, list three good things that have happened today.

My own three today have been:

1) I didn't need a coat for the first time this year.

2) I gave a small and inexpensive bunch of flowers to someone and it really seemed to cheer them up.

3) My daughter put a ludicrous bow in the dog's fur and it looked, well, ludicrous, but also incredibly sweet.

Once I started listing I realized there were lots more: I let a car in in front of me and the driver smiled; I bit into an apple that was delicious (apples can be a toss-up, quite often fuzzy and disappointing); I booked the service engineer for the dishwasher, something I have been putting off for weeks; I did more work on my current project than I thought I would … and your list will be even longer!

All good things to break those negative thought patterns.

Good Bread

I grew up in a world of sliced white and can still remember the shock when I came to London at 16 and encountered unsliced granary bread. It was warm from the baker's oven, nutty flavoured with a darkened crust and entirely delicious. Bread would never be the same again.

Even more amazing was that it was Sunday and the bread had just been baked. In the small town where I grew up shops weren't open on Sundays, and certainly no baker's – this was long before supermarkets started baking their own bread on the premises – so this granary bread summed up both new horizons of taste and city sophistication for me.

A few years ago I went to the wedding of a famous cookery writer and the bread that accompanied the lunch was another miracle: focaccia with olives, rosemary and sea salt; crusty porous ciabatta stuffed with sun-dried tomatoes or crumbled with Italian sausage. I thought I'd died and gone to bread heaven.

Since then one of life's great pleasures has been looking for the perfect bread: the narrow crunchy-cased delight of the French *ficelle* (even nicer than its often tasteless cousin the *baguette*), *pain aux noix* made with walnuts, British cottage loaves with their crazy granny-like topknots, American sourdough, Irish soda bread.

Friends tell me of the enormous pleasure of baking their own, with or without bread-makers.

And the best thing is, this is one area where the traditional has got better in modern life!

Buying Yourself Flowers

In a perfect world all of us would receive a single red rose from our husband or lover on Valentine's Day, a bouquet from our friends every birthday and a bunch of daffodils from our children to say thank you for being a wonderful mother.

Sadly, the truth is rather different, which is why the only person who will get you the flowers you deserve is you.

Personally, I feel flowers are more of an essential than a luxury. Flowers are like sunshine or familiar music – they instantly lift your mood. The greatest pleasure of all is to pick them from your own garden. You don't need many. Just a couple of roses stuck in a jug look great.

Recently the big supermarkets have started doing reasonably priced flower arrangements. The best value are those that contain gerberas, daisies and small white or green chrysanthemums, because these last well beyond their sell-by dates and can even be bought reduced and still stay alive for a week or more.

Another tip is to always cut the stems by a centimetre and soak them in flower food as soon as you get them home. If the weather's hot, place them in as cool a spot as possible. Most flowers don't like the heat.

If you have a party or big occasion coming up, it's a real experience to visit a wholesale flower market where you can buy flowers for about a third of the shop price. You don't need to be a florist, though it can be rather overwhelming to be surrounded by row after row of beautiful blooms, so you do need a clear idea of what you're after.

I also have a vulgar weakness for silk flowers, some of which are now incredibly lifelike. But there's nothing like the real thing!

Clean Sheets

Is there anything on earth as satisfying as slipping between newly laundered, crisp, clean sheets?

I have a few foibles here. I like them to be pure cotton, if possible, and by preference white with a white duvet cover, but I'm prepared to make allowances.

Hotels have a knack of making sheets smoother and crisper than you can at home – one of the special joys of staying in one, I find.

I once stayed in a hotel that had a special pillow selection that they brought round on a trolley. But for me, pillows aren't as important as the smooth embrace of freshly laundered cotton.

A Girls' Night Out

No matter how happy you are with your partner there is nothing on earth to lift the spirits like a Girls' Night Out.

It's a cliché that women turn to girlfriends for support in a crisis, but they also turn to them to have fun.

The best girly occasions are the ones where there is endless opportunity to chat, compare notes and make revelations you'd never do elsewhere. When a friend recently had a hen party in the private room of a smart restaurant, she went round the table and made everyone say their name and what they were doing in life. This could have been a deeply competitive, even divisive idea, because some of the women were high fliers, while others had reached stalemate in their lives. When the first woman began to speak I thought, 'Oh God, everyone's going to end up hating each other and feeling terrible.' In fact it turned out to be funny, honest and uplifting. Even the high fliers admitted to problems and the people whose lives were stuck could see that everything wasn't that awful after all. Of course, the champagne helped!

My husband points out wryly that Boys' Nights Out are now disapproved of, while the female version is celebrated – but then we've got a lot of catching up to do.

I also love the fairly new (in this country at least) idea of hen weekends where all the women in the group dress the same, as cowgirls or Wonder Woman or lady pirates. I assume these outings are pre-wedding. They look an awful lot of fun.

Leaving 10 Minutes Early

This is a hard one to put into practice because for some reason fate conspires against you and the very moment you are about to leave for a crucial appointment the phone rings, your keys mysteriously bury themselves in the waste bin and you realize you've forgotten to write down the address of where you're going!

By leaving 10 minutes early you give yourself the incredibly precious gift of not being stressed. You even may have time for a relaxed cappuccino (and its froth) instead of a racing heart, a sense of failure at your own inefficiency and a nasty attack of high anxiety.

Doing Something You've Been Putting Off

I know this sounds like torture rather than pleasure, but actually it works.

F. Scott Fitzgerald said that happiness was the relief after extreme tension, and that may explain why you get the most pleasure from making yourself do something you've been really dreading.

The pleasure comes in that a) you've done it at all and b) it usually wasn't as bad as you thought and possibly c) you've achieved some kind of result. But oddly enough, even if you haven't achieved much, the mere act – making the call, having it out with someone, risking failure – can make you giddy with relief and pinging with excitement.

This technique also works if the task is simply boring. You still feel good, even if it isn't quite the euphoria that's brought on by completing the scary task.

Even tiny tasks you've been really putting off can give you disproportionate pleasure when you finally *do* them. It's often effective to do them first thing in the morning. That way you can spend the rest of the day glowing with pride at your own bravery.

Looking for Shells

There is something utterly magical about finding a perfect shell. The shapes are always beautiful and satisfying and the opalescence of the best ones makes them feel like the treasure of the sea.

And no matter how old you are, it's hard to resist putting a conch to your ear expecting to hear the sound of the sea in it.

I once visited a Scottish island where the entire beach was made up of tiny cowrie shells, and have also spent many happy hours on Captiva Island, an old-fashioned and traditional part of Florida where the shells are breathtaking. The best ones are blown in by storms and I'll never forget the sight of people in the water, fully clothed, in the pouring rain of a sudden tropical storm, with umbrellas up, staring downwards as they hunted for shells.

Aaron Spelling, the TV mogul, apparently used to get his children's nanny to plant shells along the beach so that his kids could find them – cheating, rather, as the fun of shell-seeking is finding your own!

Shells are also lovely to keep. They remind you of holidays past and somehow always look absolutely perfect in bathrooms.

Opaque Tights

It's a deeply held theory of mine that black opaque tights did as much for women's career advancement as the Equal Pay Act.

OK, OK, let me explain. Black opaque tights used only to be worn by nurses, accompanied by those clumpy school-type shoes, but then they were discovered and taken over by career women.

Their appeal was that they let you wear short skirts to work without sending out the wrong signals. Women in their droves abandoned long frumpy skirt-lengths and unflattering trouser suits in favour of mini-skirts with thick tights. They still looked professional, but with opaque tights the look was professional career woman rather than, well, the other sort of professional. There was a look – long jacket, short skirt, thick black tights – that became the virtual uniform of the modern career woman for decades.

At the same time their confidence soared because

they were able to take on a man's world yet still look feminine.

And all thanks to a simple development in panty hose!

Broken Things That Suddenly Work Again

In the 1930s M. R. James wrote a famous essay called 'The Malice of Inanimate Objects'. We all know the kind of thing – the washing machine that breaks down at the worst possible moment, the car that won't start before a vital meeting, the printer that malfunctions when you have a crucial document to print. It's as if these machines actually know how much it matters and decide to break down deliberately.

But on the other side of the equation are the things that suddenly work again – for no apparent reason. The computer that announced 'Fatal error' is perfectly OK minutes later. The car mysteriously starts again. The tumble dryer whirrs into unexpected action.

And all without you getting a man in.

You feel as if someone has given you a gift. And in a way they have – the gift of not having to pay the man you would have called in. And not having to give up your valuable time worrying and telephoning the man and then waiting for the man to arrive.

Overall it's a pretty good present.

Filling in a Calendar or Diary

There's a certain moment in each year when the next one arrives – usually much earlier than you expect. Round about September I already find some dates for the following year are starting to force their attentions on me.

One reaction this produces is blind panic – the sense that time is speeding up, the seasons evaporating before I've even had time to notice they've arrived. I want the whole thing to stop.

Then I buy a calendar or diary and suddenly everything calms into a quiet pleasure. Life, I recognize, is a continuum. Yet the continuum is made up not of notable events like Big Bang or the discovery of evolution, but of term times and parents' birthdays and six-monthly dental appointments. Life has a shape. And small and domestic though the shape may sometimes be, it's rewarding and comforting.

Next year has a beginning, a middle and an end. Even though it hasn't arrived yet.

Cleaning Windows

Maybe it's the symbolism. You take a smeary, murky window, covered in cobwebs or children's sticky finger marks, get out your window-cleaning spray and hey, presto, sunlight floods into a shiny new world.

I'm not recommending you get up a ladder and do the whole house; just tackle the downstairs ones. They're the ones people notice anyway, and I'm all for cutting corners where housework's concerned.

Simple, but oh-so-satisfying.

Except, of course, if you miss a bit.

A New Magazine

You know you shouldn't.

You know it probably isn't worth it. You'll finish the thing in no time and probably it won't be worth the cover price.

The fact is, though, that magazines fill that perfect magazine-sized gap in your desires. A novel would be too long, or maybe even too improving. But a magazine! Twenty minutes of frivolous fun. And the delight in finding one that captures your interest. Whether it's the high fashion of *Vogue* or *Elle*, the gossipy pomposity of *Hello*, the peering-over-your-neighbour's-shoulder appeal of downmarket chat magazines or just drooling over other people's kitchens, there's nothing that can rival the particular pleasure of the periodical.

It's no coincidence that we associate glossy magazines with going to the hairdresser's, that other haven of indulgence and escape. I can remember how my mother, a busy doctor, looked forward to her weekly shampoo and set so that she could bury herself without guilt in a huge pile of *Woman's Own*s. Personally, at the hairdresser's I am quite promiscuous. I read all the magazines I wouldn't normally buy, dipping into the absurdly wonderful world of high fashion, the chilly and impossibly chic room-sets of *Interiors* and even the men's magazines like *Loaded* or *GQ*. To try and understand the male mind, of course.

But the greatest pleasure of all is the private one when I sit at the kitchen table, cup of coffee to hand, and open up one of the few magazines I really love, feeling the glossy finish beneath my fingertips and knowing I'm in for a quarter of an hour of sheer indulgence.

Making Satisfying Economies

It's rather rewarding that in order to be green you have to be mean. I am forever turning off lights and radiators left blazing by the rest of my family, at least as much to cut back on bills as to save the planet – though fortunately it has the same effect.

There was once a much-prized, old-fashioned saying in our grandparents' day of 'make do and mend'. Socks were darned, hems turned, hats redecorated (Jane Austen is full of old hats being trimmed with new flowers). My aunt collected old butter papers for greasing baking tins and my granny collected pieces of string and stored them in the kitchen drawer in case they might come in useful. Now we live in an age of planned obsolescence where we're told it's cheaper to throw things away than to try and mend them.

There used to be an old man round the corner from me who could mend anything – lamps, table legs that had become detached, old radios, even the bamboo handle on a holiday handbag I'd broken. It was his particular delight to say he could mend anything I brought him. Sadly few people like this remain and we throw away cameras, lights and anything electronic rather than try and mend them. Mending them may be uneconomic – but you never feel the pleasure of breathing life back into a serviceable object.

On the other hand my brother-in-law had a microwave he got in 1984; now there's a small pleasure for you – an object that actually lasts.

Wearing Sunglasses

It's hard to think of another item that confers such instant glamour. Sunglasses give the most ordinary of us mystery and allure. We are Audrey Hepburn. We are Jackie O. Put on a pair of sunglasses and we actually *feel* like a film star, sexy and desirable, even if we are only nipping down to the supermarket.

Every real celebrity hides behind them too – the bigger, the better – flashing their gold Chanel logos and their Dolce & Gabbana icons.

I welcome the arrival of summer not just because it heralds long balmy evenings and lazy days at the beach but because finally I can put on my sunglasses!

Warm Towels

It's taken me a good portion of my life to get to the stage where I have heated rails that produce gorgeous warming, enveloping, reassuring, caressing towels, the next best thing on this earth to a mother's hug.

Maybe that's why warm towels are quite so special – they do feel like a loving embrace and they probably remind all of us of that very special interlude – bath time – when we did get our mum's love and attention. Mothers and children both love bath time – children because their mothers are present (not daring to leave them) and mothers because they know this signals the end of the day and their little darlings will soon be going to bed.

Personally, I like my towels to be a little rough. The poet Rupert Brooke wrote of 'the rough male kiss of blankets' and I feel a bit the same about towels. I hate them when they've come out of the tumble dryer, all soggy and non-absorbing. The best towels have dried on the line. My teenage daughters would disagree. Softness is their special luxury and they hate the rough texture I crave in towels – a good reason for them not to use my bathroom!

In adult life the bathroom is a sanctuary, a place where you can get away from everyone and everything and indulge yourself. Most women, when they need 'me time', run straight to the bathroom and shower or soak, often with scented candles, sweet music and (a nice modern addition this) perhaps a novel and a glass of chilled Sauvignon – bliss!

There is something reassuringly ritualistic – almost like a temple ceremony – about all the immersing and anointing that happens in the bathroom and that never fails to bring balm to the spirit.

Being Met from a Journey

There is something wonderful about being met. Seeing a familiar face standing behind a barrier smiling, ready to take your bag and drive you home, is one of life's great delights. You feel loved, welcomed and part of something.

This is such a strong instinct that we tend to feel the wish to be met even when no one knows we are arriving. Not one soul on the planet may be aware what time and from what airport we are due to arrive and yet, deep in some subconscious part of ourselves, we will still be hoping to see a loved one standing there waving.

A corollary of this is having someone wave goodbye to you. One friend always makes a point of standing out in the street waving until you are out of sight, no matter how late the hour or how awful the weather. And it always has the effect of sending you off with a warm feeling inside.

Buying Shoes

Buying shoes offers a pleasure quite different from buying clothes. Perhaps it's the fact that in principle they're sensible necessary things, but they can also be frivolous luxuries.

Quite sensible down-to-earth people, in my experience, can suddenly confess to a near shoe-fetish that involves them buying a pair at every possible opportunity. Often they keep these purchases beautifully displayed in a wardrobe so that they can fling open the doors at any moment and survey their treasures.

Often it's women who have to conform in their daily dress who go in for the wildest, tartiest, most expensive flights of Jimmy Choo madness in their off-duty lives.

The truth is, every woman has a little Imelda Marcos in her and it's one of life's great pleasures to forget about the VISA bills and let herself run riot.

Cheap Jewellery

They say diamonds are a girl's best friend, but personally I think diamonds are very ageing! They make me think of 90-year-old dowagers and kept women. How much better to buy lovely, garish, cheapie stuff made from coloured glass or fake pearls or brightly coloured shells or beads!

So many craftspeople and hip young designers are creating jewellery that works because of its stylish design rather than its value. And you don't have to worry about insuring it or losing it.

When I got married in a romantic Scottish castle I didn't want a conventional headdress, I wanted a red tiara. I couldn't find one anywhere until I came across a red glass bracelet in a tiny shop on the Ile de la Cité in Paris that sold knick-knacks and tourist stuff. I asked them to make me one. They were very unsure at first, but eventually did so, and it was fabulous. It cost a tenth of a conventional tiara and was much more memorable.

The best thing about cheap jewellery is that you can buy loads of it – a necklace for every outfit – and still not worry about your bank manager pursuing you. You own and define the jewellery instead of the jewellery being too valuable for you to actually enjoy wearing it.

Throwing Coins into a Fountain

I'm not sure of the historical origins of this one, or just why good luck should follow, but it's satisfying all the same. It's an act of sheer optimism, I suppose. It must key into our need for ritual and the belief that in some way we can affect the future.

Making a wish when you cut a birthday cake and when you pull the 'wishbone' in a chicken are similar acts of crazy optimism.

I'm also a great believer in lighting candles in church, even though I lapsed from my religious belief many years ago. There is something perfect about the symbolism of a candle, a light in the darkness.

I still feel hopeful when a black cat crosses my path and wait for the good luck to follow.

An old lady friend of mine used to be a mine of *bad* luck signs – never putting shoes on the table because it meant someone had died, never mixing red and white flowers (again presaging death), never picking blossom (the fruit can't follow from the blossom if you pick it and that's bad luck)… She had hundreds of them.

Much more uplifting to believe in signs and symbols of good luck than bad!

Learning Something from Your Child

As a parent you seem to be biologically programmed to protect, teach and shelter your children from all the hurts and harms life can offer. Some parents, as Freud would point out, do this until their children are about 40 and create terrible problems for them.

Learning to let go is one of the hardest lessons parents have to learn, but there is one very special moment that helps start the process off: when you discover that this child to whom you have imparted all your wisdom, knowledge and life lessons (or tried to) actually knows something you don't. And I'm not talking technology here. We know all children over three months can programme videos, download software etc. etc.

One example was when my son showed me how you squash a bagel flat to fit it into the toaster. Another was my daughter telling me there are less than 300 calories in a skinny Starbucks peach and raspberry muffin (and they taste good too). And the moment that made me sniff a little with emotion was when my other daughter revealed that Karl Marx never actually said 'Workers of the world unite, you have nothing to lose but your chains.' Apparently it's an inaccurate translation.

You feel your work here is done!

Pashminas

There are some objects that become so much a part of everyday living that you can't imagine existing without them.

I would put pizza in this category. And central heating. Automatic gearboxes. TV remote controls. Pesto. Personal sound systems.

Pitta bread. Takeaway lattes.

And pashminas.

The fashion gurus may have decreed that pashminas are *passé*. That no self-respecting woman with a smidgen of chic would be seen dead in one. But actually millions of extremely live and lively women use them every day. They can be wraps in summer, lending decorum to skimpy summer dresses, or covering up wobbly tops of arms or rather too much middle-aged bosom. In winter they become scarves. One of my daughters showed me how to wrap them in that clever way that makes them look smart instead of provincial. They add a splash of glorious colour to a grey world. The pashmina palette runs from aqua to sugar-almond pink and daring scarlet to trendy taupe. They come in gauze for summer and cashmere for winter.

Is there any other fashion item as versatile as a pashmina?

A Sexy Massage

Sometimes you feel too tired to offer a massage to your beloved. Sometimes – let's be honest – you think, 'I've just changed the duvet. Do I want to risk getting massage oil on my nice clean sheets?'

But sexy massages really work. They make your partner feel sensual and appreciated and you feel wonderful when they return the favour.

Sexy massages fall into that bracket of faintly naughty activity that releases fantasies and reminds even people who know each other well that they possess parts of the body they'd almost forgotten about!

Tasks with an Echo of the Past

Once, when I was hanging washing on a line, I wondered why this was a task that seemed to give an extra-special sense of satisfaction. The sun was shining and there was a fresh wind, the kind of breeze our grandmothers would have called 'a good drying wind'. Hanging each item, smoothing it out, then pegging it, had a curiously enjoyable rhythm which surprised me, because to be frank I normally use a tumble dryer! There was also a great sense of pleasure in finding a couple of hours later that the washing was bone-dry and smelt delicious, with none of that fake aroma of 'Spring Breeze' you get from fabric conditioners. Even folding the sheets (two people, preferably one at each end) was enjoyable.

I realized that there were other small repetitive tasks that also gave deep pleasure – pulling curtains, topping and tailing fruit, making beds with neat hospital corners, collecting eggs from chickens, even doing the washing-up with a woman friend or relative where you have to match your speed with theirs. And I realized that some actions have echoes with the past; they are the kind of communal women's tasks that have been done for generations and have often been lost in the rush and stress of modern life.

Modern urban men probably feel the same when they find themselves chopping wood. The task, pleasurable in itself, reverberates with echoes of the past and this provides even deeper enjoyment.

Women once used to sing as they wove or sewed in groups, like the tweed makers of the Shetland Isles of Scotland, and some of that communal experience seems to transmit itself to this day. These small everyday actions seem to link us to the past in a deep unconscious way, and that's why we gain such intense pleasure from them.

Letting Someone into Traffic

It's so easy not to. So easy to be mean, to tell yourself you're in a hurry, you'll be late and you need to get there double-quick. So you avoid the eyes of the other driver and stick close to the car in front.

Behind you, someone else lets them in. And then you wonder, 'Why did I do that?'

Next time you let them in. And they give you a big wide hugging smile. You feel great. Kind. Generous. Big-hearted. But you won't always let them in next time.

Maybe it's because we're only human.

Not Getting a Parking Ticket

You know the feeling. You should have gone back to your car 10 minutes ago. Or maybe you should have paid for longer in the first place. But you didn't.

Anyway, now you're late. As you run back to the car you visualize the ticket on your windscreen. Or the sight of the parking warden writing it out as you return, shrugging and saying there's nothing they can do about it.

It'll mean a hefty fine. And it's not just that it'll be a waste of money and you'll feel stupid. What about all the things you could have done with the money instead?

You turn the corner and there's your car.

It hasn't got a ticket.

You grin. It's almost like being given a present.

You know you shouldn't have taken the risk.

And that you'll do it again.

But this time you got away with it.

Flirting

Flirting, an art in the 1920s and '30s, has gone out of fashion, to be replaced by that awful expression 'networking'. Yet anyone who's indulged in a slightly forbidden romance knows how life can be transformed by the presence of the Other.

Flirting makes the heart beat faster. It makes the eyes brighter, the hair shinier, the body trimmer. It hones your repartee and lightens your step.

The crucial question is, does flirtation have to lead to an affair or is it a satisfactory end in itself? Maybe I'm being naïve, but I would say it can be pleasantly harm-free, providing you know where to draw the line.

In fact, I'd go further and say you don't even have to meet to flirt. I've had enjoyable mini-flirts over the phone with hotel booking clerks, car servicing managers and even an Internet helpdesk agent.

Providing you're having a light-hearted laugh, a mild flirtation reminds you that you're an attractive and desirable being. Even if you happen to be happily married to someone else.

Flirting is like adding cinnamon to a baked apple – it isn't necessary, but it adds an exciting touch of spice.

Hotel Toiletries

I don't know about you, but the number-one way I judge hotels is by their free toiletries. Forget five stars and excellent room service, do they have delicious little bottles of shampoo and free bath gel?

The best toiletries I've come across were by Annick Goutal, but I'm happy to settle for The Body Shop or Penhaligon's.

I always pinch the lot every day, telling myself they're for my children, but actually they're for me. To me a bath without bath gel is like champagne without bubbles.

Once, in a boutique hotel in SoHo, New York, there was a condom nestling amongst the freebies with a label saying: 'Enjoy yourself safely.' I thought it was so funny I took it home to show my daughters!

Drinking from Your Favourite Cup

Sitting at your kitchen table, looking out at the sunshine, drinking coffee or tea from your favourite cup… Life doesn't get much better than that.

My cousin insists that tea should only be drunk from china. There's something about the marriage of tea and the thin translucency of china that makes the brew taste entirely different, she says.

China and pottery are doubly enjoyable because you can both use and collect them. I now own half of the beautiful Mason's Ironstone dinner service my mother collected. I can remember as a little girl being allowed to put the bread roll on the side plates before her dinner guests arrived and feeling incredibly privileged and grown-up. And now I own the side plates

Part of the allure of china and pottery, I think, is that they are objects that have significance beyond their everyday use. In America we once visited a shipwreck museum and I still remember the tea crates rescued from the ocean bed, neatly packed with straw, filled with somebody's best china. I could just imagine a young woman, maybe having to leave her homeland, stowing away her most precious items deep in the chest, hoping to unpack them in an entirely new life. And here they were, on display, 300 years later. I always hoped she hadn't drowned.

The special appeal of china is that it can be both useful and beautiful. I love collecting china jugs, either to put milk or cream in or to fill with bunches of flowers. One of my favourites is an absolutely plain white milk jug which looks as if it has come straight from a dairy. It's just like one that Tess of the d'Urbervilles might have used in Thomas Hardy's wonderful nineteenth-century novel. Even plain china has a romance of its own.

Talking to Shopkeepers

Part of the reason we all get so depressed nowadays, even though we're materially better off than ever before, is isolation from families, neighbours and communities. One of the simplest and most life-enhancing ways to re-establish contact with your surroundings is to talk to people who work in shops.

Recently when I decided to do this I discovered that my greengrocer, whom I'd bought my leeks from for years, was a Greek Cypriot who supported Spurs football club, that the local florist had been set up in business (with his boyfriend) by his mum and that the wine shop and café/bakery were run by French people. There was a thriving Parisian community in the area, the wine-shop manager told me, and it was well known in Paris as a nice place to live! I was amazed that all this could have been going on without my even noticing!

Ever since then I've made a point of talking to all the shopkeepers nearby and shopping has become a much more enjoyable, even adventurous, experience. And it's also made me feel much more a part of my community.

Matching Underwear

A Parisian friend of mine, when I explained my new-found delight in matching underwear, looked at me wide-eyed. '*Cherie*,' she enquired, 'is there any other kind?'

Well, yes. For me, anyway. My underwear drawer used to resemble the cast-offs from a vicarage jumble sale – greying knickers, ancient bras, mouldy tights and one or two raunchier items purchased with the aim of spicing up my sex life and rarely, if ever, used, plus the odd unmatching popsock.

Then I discovered lingerie sets. Bliss! Now I am permanently primed for either a passionate and unexpected affair or being run over on a zebra crossing (a great preoccupation of my granny's).

Wearing Flip-flops

From basic plastic ones to high-fashion items in gold leather made by Gucci, I love them all.

Perhaps their appeal is the simplicity of the design or the fact that the same simple object is worn by chic and unchic alike. Either way, flip-flops are a magnificent invention. Even the sound of them slapping on the ground as you walk makes me think instantly of Greek beaches and brilliant blue skies.

This year they have been the height of fashion, worn by chic girls in posh frocks, but when the fashion-conscious have dumped them in the bin they will still be with us – on the feet of urchins offering to watch your car for you and of men in shorts of every age.

Unblocking Loos

Just to show this book is not all about flowers and candles and wall-to-wall pampering, here's a reminder of nature's more basic side.

An ancient plumber gave me this tip when I called him out to a loo jammed up with about two toilet rolls' worth of loo paper. I won't describe the scene. Most unpleasant.

The man got out his tools and solved the problem in moments.

'Would we need a special rod like this,' I asked him, 'to do the deed ourselves?'

He shook his head and smiled. Did we have an old-fashioned mop? The kind made not of shredded J-cloths but bits of string attached to a long handle?

We did indeed.

'Shove it down the loo until it entirely fills the bowl

down to the S-bend,' he commanded, 'then – plop – pull it quickly out.'

It worked like magic. Now I keep a store of those old mops in case they stop making them. In fact, I have become the S-Bend Queen.

And, I have to admit, I feel out-of-proportionally proud each time I manage to do it single-handedly.

Getting a Tan

We know it's bad for us. We know it ages skin, promotes melanoma and is horribly self-destructive.

And yet we do it.

People look better with a tan. Fashion editors may write features on 'Pale is Beautiful', but we go to the Tanning Shop or lie out like mad dogs and Englishmen in the midday sun.

Because we feel better with a tan. We feel slimmer. Sexier. Younger (even though our skin is older).

From time to time we listen to the good advice and stay out of the sun. But we still want a tan. So we use fake stuff. We stand in cubicles being sprayed with evil-smelling lotions.

But it isn't the same. It looks orange. It comes off on our clothes. Besides, we don't get that feeling of warmth and wellbeing.

People aren't called sun-worshippers for nothing. There is something ritualistic about lying down, eyes closed, and feeling your skin warming up that is satisfying at some deep primeval level.

Maybe we're descended from lizards?

Granny's Tips

There used to be a radio programme where people phoned in with their handy tips and hints, the kind of thing that would once have been handed on from mother to daughter. The callers were mostly old ladies suggesting 1,001 uses for old tights, from stuffing toys with them to using them to catch snails.

Some of the tips were just useful pieces of information: removing grease stains by ironing with brown paper; eating local honey to stop hayfever allergy; using toothpaste instead of calamine lotion for stings; running your hands over the metal of a tap to stop them smelling of garlic or onions.

My mother added one that I still follow: *Always keep enough money on you for a taxi home.* I used to keep it in my knee-length boots when they were fashionable and have occasionally stuffed it in my bra!

It was such good advice that I have handed it on to my daughters.

Opening your Mail

I love that magical sound of the post dropping onto the doormat. You know it will probably be all bills or letters from the tax inspector. But maybe it won't. Perhaps there will be a cheque. Or an invitation. A thank-you card or a catalogue from a favourite clothes company you can enjoy over a cup of coffee.

It's worth remembering how much pleasure things like this give us. That way we can remember to send nice messages to other people too.

I feel nearly as much pleasure (though not quite as much) at opening e-mails.

Holiday Reading

Is there anything nicer than stretching out in a sun-lounger on the first day of your holiday and opening a brand-new book which you have bought especially for holiday reading?

It might be by Camus or Jackie Collins. Stendhal or Danielle Steele. Whatever it is, it somehow sums up the me-time feeling of holidays when for once you sit down on a weekday and lose yourself in the world the writer has created.

It always amazes me that some holidaymakers can just lie, completely still, eyes closed, unmoving in the sun for hour after hour. For me, holidays are about books.

Even if it does mean you end up with an irritating white stripe down your neck where the book cast a shadow!

Decluttering

Every woman's magazine or self-help guide assures us that decluttering is the key to life. An uncluttered living space leads, like a white dove released into a clear blue sky, to a free spirit and untrammelled thinking. At least that's what they tell us.

Charity shops will explain that there are seasons for decluttering, depending on the weather and on sudden impulses to turn out wardrobes and decide if we can possibly get away with wearing our favourite baggy trousers for another year. Not surprisingly, spring is number-one season for decluttering.

We also live in a society where minimalism is currently all the rage. In Victorian times, the more possessions you could cram into a room, the more admired it would be. Aspidistras, knick-knacks, souvenirs, fans, pianos… Now it's the opposite. Glossy magazines are full of Japanese-inspired emptiness. Each possession must be selected with care, and woe betide you if it's the wrong shade for the décor. And paintings are chosen less for their challenging content than for whether they match the curtains.

Of course there's a lot of satisfaction in transforming your home from an eclectic mish-mash to a harmonious neutral-tinted whole and we all feel a soaring sense of satisfaction at taking eight black bin bags to the charity shop. At least our mistakes might be another person's good fortune. But in my view it can all go too far.

Fortunately, Real Life invariably intrudes. Carpets are walked on by boys in muddy trainers. Sofas are sat on. Cushions are crumpled. Homework spreads itself like a creeper across stylish oak dining tables.

Which is how it should be. And explains the next small pleasure on the list.

Recluttering

Minimalism may be the flavour of the month, but it does go against some dyed-in-the-wool human instincts. There are certainly joys in stripping your home (or your life) down to essentials, but what do you do about those two great human instincts: getting and spending?

Girls love shopping for clothes, women love shopping for – well, quite a lot of things. One moment we hate capitalism and its need to create desires in us we didn't even know we had. We want to empty our lives, we want to simplify. Then we wander into some gorgeous kitchen shop, or fashionable boutique, or dear little village gift shoppe, and in ten seconds flat out with the plastic and we've bought something! And sometimes these little somethings are wonderful. They remind us of a person we love, or a treasured experience, or we just want them, dammit! And abracadabra, our lives are cluttered again.

There's no point feeling guilty about it. Enjoy it!

Acquiring is a human instinct. Any visit to a museum will demonstrate how the Greeks, Egyptians, Romans and Etruscans all made pretty things as well as useful ones, and you can bet your last sesterce that they collected things whether they needed them or not.

OK, the Greek philosopher Diogenes *was* famous for having no possessions and living in a barrel in the streets of Athens. When the emperor Alexander the Great offered him any gift he wanted on earth, he replied, 'You can get out of my sun.'

Few of us could aspire to Diogenes's downshifted state, but maybe we can have great fun cluttering, decluttering and cluttering again.

Using the Internet

I absolutely adore the Internet. In fact, I can't imagine how we ever existed before it. I know it has a somewhat grubby image of lots of sad and isolated people hunched over their lonely computers, but I suspect the truth is the opposite. It is a real modern community. I love reading people's blogs, hearing about their everyday lives across the globe and getting their own personal advice on everything from how to avoid the midnight munchies and survive broken romances to how to remove stubborn grease stains using only lemon juice and elbow grease. I love booking flights as easily as ordering a taxi. I love all the information I can access – everything from finding out whether Humphrey Bogart really did say 'Play it again, Sam' to viewing detailed floor plans of medieval monasteries.

The Internet is quite simply a miracle. It even revives lost friendships between busy people. I am sure many people would say their lives were enriched emotionally by being able to keep in contact with distant friends and family via the net in a way never achieved by the annual round-robin letter.

The Internet also keeps you continually in touch. When my elder daughter spent three months in Shanghai recently, I talked to her more often via e-mail than I ever do when she's in the next room.

Of all the modern inventions I can think of, the Internet is (despite all those scares about porn and paedophiles) the most potentially life-enriching. I don't buy the idea that life was better when we talked over the garden wall rather than via the Internet. Those days had gone before the web even arrived. In fact it has given us a global wall to lean over and chat.

And I for one am more than happy to do so.

New Yorker Cartoons

I love the sophistication of them.

When I was growing up my father subscribed to the *New Yorker*. (This was pretty unusual in our small town in the south of England.) In those days I used to read the cartoons with blank incomprehension. *New Yorker* cartoons are far too grown-up for a 10-year-old to get. Even a modern 10-year-old.

Now I still don't get some of them, but mostly I think they're wonderful. Recently the magazine has marketed them as birthday cards and I find they're often the funniest around.

This year I gave my husband one I especially liked. It featured a large male leopard sitting in an armchair watching TV. Behind him the female leopard, wearing a pinny, is saying, 'I didn't ask you to change your spots. Just to put the garbage out.'

Another favourite of mine features two snails looking at an identically shaped Sellotape dispenser. One is saying, 'I don't *care* if she's a tape dispenser, I still love her!'

Somehow it manages to be oddly touching.

Sinking into New-mown Grass

It's a summer evening in the small provincial town where I grew up. Somewhere in the distance I can hear the thwack of tennis balls. The lawn has just been cut and there is a huge pile of new-mown grass. I throw myself into its warm moist embrace. It smells like nothing else on earth – green and tender and fresh.

Even now, as an adult, the scent of new-mown grass stops me in my tracks and transports me back to the enticing world of childhood where everything seemed sunny and suburban and safe. Those golden days before adulthood and having to make difficult decisions…

One of my grandmothers always wore 4711 Eau de Cologne, the other English Lavender Water, and a dab of those will bring either granny sharply into focus. Sadly, both perfumes are barely available now, a pity because Lavender Water, I'm told, is lethally effective against mosquitoes. Perhaps that is why my grandmother, who lived for many years in India, loved it so.

There are other scents that have the same effect: ripe peaches, sweet peas, russet apples, ink, freshly laundered sheets, beach tar, mothballs, woollen jumpers drying out, Parma violet sweets… All these take me straight back to childhood. And there is enormous pleasure in closing your eyes and letting yourself be transported. So, close your eyes, awaken your senses and jump…

Giving Advice

There is a special thrill in giving advice. It means you are the one with the wisdom and power, the One Who Has Not Screwed Up. Since the person you are giving it to is admitting they need it (unless you're giving it whether they want it or not, a dangerous game unless you are their mother), you are necessarily in a superior position.

Unfortunately, giving advice can easily be motivated by one-upmanship (or more commonly one-upwomanship) masquerading as kindness or down-to-earth common sense. And the heady pleasures of being the one with the wisdom can make you quite insensitive. Perhaps it's better to recognize that the thrill of giving advice should be its own reward and to remember that people who *really* think they know how other people should behave are pretty insufferable.

You also have to accept that the person you're advising is very unlikely to take your advice. People tend to do what they want, not what other people think they should do, however wise or well-meant the counsel.

And life always has a trick up its sleeve, and soon you could be having advice dished out to you.

So give advice gently.

The Song of the Chainsaw

I know this may sound a bit weird, and possibly like the preamble to a horror film by Stephen King, but actually the buzz of the chainsaw is one of the first sounds of spring.

It arrives even before that other sign of spring, the hum of the first lawnmower. I often sit up and listen to it, occasionally opening my window to do so, because even though it's still cold and technically winter, this sound always cheers me up. If the chainsaw is whining, can spring be far behind?

Even better, after a few days of hearing chainsaws in neighbouring gardens I know we are approaching that crucial moment of spiritual renewal: a day so warm and pleasant you just have to go outside. Without understanding fully why, you'll find yourself sweeping the patio, mowing the lawn or just taking a cup of coffee out into the garden. Another spring has begun!

Friends

Friends have to be one of the most vital, wonderful, all-encompassing pleasures of all.

It's a modern cliché that friends are the new family. Families may fracture, or live miles away, but friends are always there for you.

I was disgusted, reading the work of a life coach recently, to find that they suggested you discarded friends who were no longer positive influences in your life. Friendship just isn't like that. We acquire friends in different ways – some from school, some from ballet classes when we were five, some through our own children. Friendship is an amazing tapestry that grows through life. Maybe, in fact, it's more of a rug than a tapestry because it can be thrown over you at terrible times and it keeps you warm and protects you when you need it most.

Life without friendship is unimaginable. It would be so much poorer an experience.

Recent research in the UK has shown that, far from discarding old friends, we are finding that friendships play a crucial part in our lives. The happiest people are those who have a variety of friends.

In fact, social relationships are generally viewed as more enriching than money. A recent survey from London's prestigious Institute of Education suggested that seeing your friends or family every day was worth as much in terms of wellbeing as an £85,000 pay rise! I've no idea how they calculated this sum, but I know exactly what they mean. The Bible might have said that a virtuous woman has a price far beyond rubies, but friends (virtuous or not) are worth even more than that!

A Crisp Apple

Apples are so wonderfully designed. Absolutely portable. You don't even have to unzip them, as you do bananas, and when they're good, they're perfect. A ripe peach, so juicy it runs down your chin, or a firm but sweet sharp raspberry is pretty divine, but there's still nothing quite like the sharp tangy deliciousness of a perfect seasonal apple.

Perhaps it's the fact that so many apples, especially imported ones, can disappoint that makes finding the one that doesn't even more thrilling.

Everyone has their personal favourite, from yellow and crunchy Golden Delicious to green and crunchy Granny Smith. My son adores Pink Lady. But for me there's only one fabulous queen of all apples: the sharp-but-sweet Cox's Orange Pippin, picked just when it ought to be in early autumn.

Eve, I forgive you. I'd have eaten the apple too.

Dancing When No One Can See You

You're loading the dishwasher or chopping an onion and suddenly, on the radio or your iPod, the most irresistible, infectious, upbeat music appears.

And you start to dance with sheer pure bodily joy.

With me it's Paul Simon when he has the Ladysmith Black Mbazo singers backing him. Or some Tamla Motown. Or Justin Timberlake. Or something unbearably corny like 'Livin' la Vida Loca'. The kind of stuff they play at wedding discos.

Oh, I just remembered my favourite for dancing joyously alone, with absolutely no one watching you: Dean Martin singing 'That's *Amore*'.

Now that's embarrassing.

Go on, admit it. What's yours?

Fresh Pesto

Every country has its little culinary miracles which are adopted by different parts of the globe for the simple reason that they work brilliantly and are delicious. A few examples would be French bread, Danish pastries, Turkish pitta and German beer.

Italy produces more of these little miracles than most: pizza, Italian ice cream, ciabatta bread, Bolognese ragu, mozzarella – and pesto, the delicious sauce made of fresh basil leaves, olive oil, pine nuts and Parmesan cheese.

Pesto works with everything – on pasta, with salads, on ciabatta in sandwiches with roasted peppers. We even have a recipe that layers pink lamb escalopes with aubergine and spinach and is finished off with a teaspoon of pesto on top. It tastes incredible and looks clever and expensive.

There's just one rule: use only fresh pesto, not the stuff in jars, which, even when it's made in Italy, always tastes of soap rather than basil.

Eating Outside

Why is it that eating outside is such a huge pleasure? Often we will queue for hours for an outdoor table in a café or restaurant, even though that table happens to be beside a noisy road right in the middle of a city!

There seems to be a huge human instinct to get into the great outdoors whenever remotely possible. Perhaps it's partly climate change, but the culture of the barbecue and the pavement café has spread everywhere.

Certain outdoor eating and drinking experiences are especially memorable – breakfast of patisseries and *café au lait* in Paris, Bellinis in St Mark's Square in Venice, scones and cream in an English tea garden, yogurt and honey in a beachside Greek café.

But the truth is, any meal tastes nicer when eaten under a wide blue sky.

Getting Invitations

There is something about receiving an invitation that is always exciting.

You can usually tell it's an invitation just from the look of the envelope. Invitations tend to look different from ordinary letters.

In Britain there is a lot of snob value attached to them – the most formal invites are written in copperplate and are embossed, not printed. Posh people are often seen running their fingers over the print to check if it's been done correctly!

When we got married we decided to follow convention by having the invitation embossed in copperplate – but we made the lettering bright pink.

Whatever they look like, invitations are always life-enhancing. Perhaps it's the Cinderella in all of us, or the fact that we love to dress up now and then even if we don't run to glass slippers, but an invitation is always cheering. It means you'll catch up with old friends or even meet new ones.

Actually, any invitation is lovely, even on-the-spot informal ones, or someone unexpectedly saying, 'Why don't you stay for a drink?'

The truth is we're social animals, and, like so many other pleasures, an invitation connects us. It says, 'How lovely to see you, don't go, why don't you stay and chat?' That's a good reason why we should be prepared to issue and accept invitations on the spot. We should stop agonizing about the quality of our cooking or the acceptability of our wine – something that puts so many people off entertaining – and just ask. It's the company people enjoy, not the *haute-cuisine* menu.

Cold Water on Your Face

I love this feeling.

Beauty experts tell you never to do it. Rubbish. It makes you feel alive and awake, even after a late night or a horribly early start.

A fellow novelist says, 'Forget your complexion, throw cold water on your boobs!' Hers have remained perky even though the rest of her body has sagged (she insists) and she is convinced this is the reason.

I think I'll just stick to my face.

Growing Sweet Peas

Like a stunning Hollywood star, sweet peas have the reputation of being beautiful but temperamental. But I – as one of the world's worst gardeners, who can kill a plant at 10 paces – can deny this from my own experience, for I have grown sweet peas. Admittedly not from seed, but from four seedlings. OK, true gardeners would scoff, but the plants positively flourished.

The amazing fact that few people know about sweet peas is that they produce a bunch of blooms a day. It is a little miracle to pick a bunch in the morning and find by the evening (if it's really sunny) that another two dozen flowers have appeared.

Sweet-pea colours are envied and imitated by endless interior designers. No other plant seems to produce quite that sugar-almond pink, pale lilac or deep Delft blue.

Sweet peas make me think of Degas ballerinas, or young Victorian misses, dressed innocently in pastels, pretty yet chaste.

And the scent! Apart from lily of the valley, no other flower has such a sweet perfume. They are quite simply in a class (or glass?) of their own.

An Object That Is Just Right for the Task

There is actually a proper name for this: appropriate technology.

This description was coined for user-friendly equipment that people feel they can actually operate without being daunted by. The fax machine was a classic. Dead simple. It worked. And it wasn't invasive, unlike the more complex stuff that followed.

But on a lesser level appropriate technology is just something that's really useful and gives you actual pleasure to use. For example, I have owned an ancient plastic kitchen scraper for more than 20 years which is handy for a score of jobs from getting the last scrape of cake mixture out of the bowl to cleaning fridges to getting stubborn bits off allegedly non-stick frying pans.

I also have a beloved fountain pen, cheap but incredibly

effective, that never blotches or lets me down; a boxed set of five IKEA tools that meet most household emergencies; Sellotape dispensers that I've hung on to for 10 years because they make Christmas wrapping so much easier; a champagne opener that takes the fear out of fizz bottles; and a leather shoulder bag that defies the vagaries of fashion but has exactly the right number of pockets for phone, make-up and car keys. Since owning it I have never, not once, had to go through that turning-out-your-bag-on-the-bonnet routine so familiar to many women (and so beloved of men since they can indulge in that superior smile).

When you have an appropriate object in your life, guard it well. Never succumb to the temptation to replace it with something fancier, more expensive and 10 times more complicated.

Birdsong

Every time we go on a country walk I bore my children with: 'Listen, can you hear that?' The teenagers roll their eyes and say, 'We know, it's another skylark.'

So far they don't seem to appreciate the sheer joyousness so clear to Shelley in his famous poem 'To a Skylark', where he recreates the sound through the interplay between the trochaic trimester and a sweeping hexameter: 'And singing still dost soar, and soaring ever singest.'

They are left cold by the familiar notes of Vaughan Williams's much-loved *Lark Ascending*.

For now.

I'm convinced that, later on, birdsong will mean as much to them as it does to me. One day, like people throughout the centuries, they will thrill at the sound of the first cuckoo, that joyous herald of spring, or even at the humble coo-coo-coo of the wood pigeon. They'll feel happy to be alive if they catch the call of the curlew or the glorious musical outpourings of the blackbird or the nightingale.

And they'll bore their own children, who will one day in turn bore theirs.

Finding You Haven't Put Weight On

OK, so you overindulged. You went away on holiday or away for the weekend somewhere delicious and romantic and had breakfast in bed and gorgeous puddings, or even stayed at home and ate too many Krispy Kreme doughnuts.

You get on the scales. You close your eyes. Maybe you even do that female thing of leaning in a special low-weight direction.

You look down. Miracle of miracles, you haven't put on a pound!

Of course, being lucky to get away with it, you should now behave sensibly and eat only what's good for you.

Or possibly have another doughnuts.

Keeping a Journal

I don't use the word 'diary'. Diaries are for appointments and have to be kept every day. They are to do with practicality and efficient time management.

Journals are altogether different, harder to pin down. They are for observations, revelations, confessions, statements of personal intent. At times they can be cries of desperation. Or ways of making resolutions, even though it's nowhere near New Year's Eve.

They are extremely helpful. Psychotherapists talk of 'journalling', which means, I suppose, coming out with the stuff you might reveal to a therapist and dealing with it yourself.

Travel journals are rewarding, too, but the kind I've got in mind are about personal rather than geographical journeys. In a journal you can tell the truth, confess a weakness, be a soggy mess.

I have always believed in writing things down, from lists of pros and cons when you have a difficult decision to make to assessing the ways in which you can improve a situation. But I don't keep my journals. As soon as they are finished, at the year's end, I read them through and throw them away. I don't want them to be read by other people. Too explosive.

Diaries are different. I have hung on to those from the last 20 years and it's interesting how useful they are when you can't remember which year you did something significant.

Diaries, unlike journals, aren't dangerous and revealing.

Things That Turn Out Better Than Expected

One of the sad things about life is that events we really look forward to – holidays, family gatherings, homecomings and reunions – can turn out worse than expected. We can lay such a weight of expectation and emotion onto them that they can have a built-in anti-climax.

But the flip side is that other events, ones we aren't looking forward to at all, can be unexpectedly wonderful.

The best things in life are actually those that surprise you – the sudden sunshine, the spontaneous supper, the unplanned invitation, the scratch meal you throw together with friends.

This is hard to accept if you happen to be a perfectionist. For instance, I used to plan holidays right down to the exact room with the very best view looking down over the turquoise sea. Until one year I booked the wrong room and it didn't have the perfect balcony with the perfect view and I realized I'd have to accept it or it would ruin my holiday. After a struggle I let it go and something amazing happened: I found I enjoyed holidays more if I stopped planning them, if I just waited to see what would happen rather than tried to get every detail right in advance.

I realized that holidays – like events – can unfold in a lot of different ways, and they can be more pleasurable for being unexpected.

Park Life

There is something endlessly uplifting about public parks. The variety of life is endless, from determined joggers and energetic dog walkers to laughing children playing football or chasing Frisbees, eager sunbathers optimistically trying to catch the rays or old men passing the hours on benches chatting about politics or the cost of living.

Perhaps it's the feeling of democracy, the idea that parks are open to one and all, that gives them their special feeling, but somehow they always cheer you up.

I even love the habit of dedicating park benches to people when they die. Each bench to 'Edwin, who loved this place' or 'Dora, beloved grandmother, much missed by her family' seems to tell a story and add a richness of shared experience that is somehow much more life-enhancing than gravestones could ever be.

Parks provide a story of ordinary people that goes on and on. Like the people who use them, they offer a living tapestry of daily life that mixes happiness, loss and tragedy. They can offer just as much solace and peace as a visit to a church, and can give a sense of the continuity of everyday life that leaves you with a sense of the preciousness of ordinary life.

Getting Something for Nothing ... or Not Much Anyway

I used to tease my mother-in-law for clipping the money-off vouchers out of newspapers, but now, with the wisdom of experience, I am a big fan of loyalty cards, BOGOFs (Buy One Get One Free) and all manner of money-off schemes.

There is a particular high in getting something for nothing (or not a lot) and these days there are endless opportunities to do so. Every newspaper, vying in life-or-death circulation wars, seems to offer cheap or free air travel or at the very least a free CD or DVD. And every time I check my e-mail, there's another Internet airline offering to fly me to some fascinating destination for about the same cost as a taxi to the airport!

There couldn't be a better time to take advantage of these seductive come-ons. Sadly, my children are still quite young, so I can't fully unleash myself onto Planet Freebie yet, but I mean to be the best-travelled empty-nester in the Western World once they leave home, unless concern about the future of the planet stops me. So unfair that cheap travel has arrived at exactly the moment fear of global warming may stop us making the most of it!

Maybe the joys of something-for-nothing are particularly sweet because a lot of the time we feel manipulated by big corporations and this is the way we claw a little something back.

Wallowing in Self-pity

We live in a culture that is dedicated to Moving On. Anyone who hasn't recovered from their relationship break-up, job loss or pet's death within three months is considered a wimp.

I view things differently. It is perfectly justifiable to wallow, make late-night phone calls to your friends, moan endlessly, hide under the bed covers and ignore all housework for as long as you need.

People are different. Some recover by pretending nothing happened. Others like to suffer in Technicolor.

The reassuring thing is that in the end most people do come out of the dark tunnel of loss and disappointment unless they are suffering from clinical depression.

And they should be given all the time in the world to do it.

Don't move on till you're ready. Buy another box of Kleenex and hit that sofa. Your friends may complain, but one day it'll be their turn too.

An Old-fashioned Dressing Table

Dressing tables were highly unfashionable when I was growing up. We were reacting against suburban 1950s kidney-shaped versions, draped in brightly coloured fabrics with frills on them. The price we paid for our disapproval was decades of putting our make-up on in the bathroom with nowhere to balance our foundation or mascara and having to lean uncomfortably over a sink to see into the mirror.

Recently there's been a romantic revival in the fortunes of dressing tables and I love it. Mine is curvy and capacious, covered in photos of friends and family in pretty photo frames. Jewellery is draped everywhere, as well as perfume, some of it in old cut-glass bottles. I haven't gone as far as feathers, but almost.

I sit on a proper stool and I can see into my mirror at exactly the right distance. My dressing table has three drawers where I can keep all my girly junk, hairdryers, anti-frizz serum, eye make-up remover and tissues.

I even have a vase of fresh roses from the garden, pink Savoy Hotel for preference, whenever I can.

And despite its rather over the top *fin-de-siècle* feel, my dressing table is deeply practical, far more so than having to perform difficult rituals using the mirror of the bathroom cabinet.

I feel like Greta Garbo or a heroine from Daphne du Maurier.

Except when my daughters, appreciating the pleasure and practicality of my dressing table, borrow it and leave all my stuff in a mess.

Then I feel more like the Wicked Witch of the West.

Having Some Running-away Money

Spending too much can be a dizzying pleasure, but an even greater one lies in keeping some money back.

There are so many situations in life that are fraught with stress: a bad relationship, a job that bores you, the threat of debt closing in. Running-away Money gives you a passport to freedom – whether actual freedom or just freedom from feeling trapped. It gives you the capacity to say 'I don't need this any more,' whether you actually choose to keep it or not. And just having capacity to choose changes things.

I have never been that interested in jewels or expensive cars, or first-class air travel. Any money I've made has meant one thing: freedom.

And even though, as yet, I've never needed my little nest egg, the fact that I know it's there makes me feel free.

Lavish Curtains

Perhaps this is one of my little obsessions, but I believe lavish curtains, generous of fabric allocation, double- or treble-widthed, tumbling wherever possible in waterfalls of fabric on the carpet, are little short of life-enhancing.

How miserable are those skimpy little curtains, unlined and barely reaching the bottom of the window sill? They speak of meanness and lack of imagination.

I know curtains are expensive, but far better to buy cheap fabrics like natural calico and have it frothing about in generous abundance than to splash out on half a metre of expensive brocade and look meagre and penny-pinching.

Once, when we couldn't afford the right fabric for a room we'd just done up, I bought two large dustsheets from a builder's yard and added some stylish tie-backs. I then tacked the lot up. They looked amazing just because they contained so much fabric – never mind the quality, the width made the effect generous and classy. No one ever guessed I'd used builder's dustsheets! The only trouble is, because they look OK it's three years on and I still haven't got round to replacing them!

Opening Shutters

Perhaps it's because shutters are unfamiliar, exotic holiday things, but I get a huge thrill from throwing them open wide. It could be because of going from darkness to light or because you expect a bright Mediterranean panorama awaiting you, but the action is always thrilling.

Perhaps shutters are a kind of metaphor for throwing open the soul.

Opening curtains doesn't have quite the same thrill of possibility, but it too has its own quiet pleasure, especially if they're on a cord that has to be pulled so that you feel almost as if you are revealing the stage of a theatre – but the theatre is your day ahead.

There's an element of drama in opening curtains. What will await you? Will it be rain or sun?

Recycling

There is a wonderful song by Nick Lowe called 'I Love the Sound of Breaking Glass'. I hear it ringing in my ears every time I drop a bottle into the recycling bin and hear that wonderfully rewarding crash.

It's legitimized vandalism, I suppose. That plus the feeling of satisfaction you get in making sure the glass from the wine you drank last night gets used again. The glow of satisfaction almost – but not quite – makes up for your guilt at the number of bottles you're putting in the recycling in the first place.

Recycling is quite a time-consuming process. As I sort out the plastic from the cardboard from the tin cans I try not to think of how having all our electrical items on standby probably more than cancels out any good all this sorting-out does for the planet.

In many ways recycling is the modern repackaging of another highly satisfying concept: thrift. Our grandparents' generation didn't have much and they kept everything: cardboard boxes, old shoes, newspapers, butter papers for baking, old pieces of string. The theory was that almost everything would come in useful some time or other. Decluttering is a truly modern post-plenty concept which few of our grandparents would either recognize or have any sympathy for.

This of course was in the days when people had lofts. The days before loft conversions took away all the spare space from houses and brought along in their wake the whole concept of minimalism.

I once made a TV programme about a family who had no rubbish at all – they managed to recycle every last scrap. I fall a long way short of that ideal.

The ultimate recycling machine is of course a pig, something every country family once had. It saved many of them from starvation.

There are limits, though.

Takeaway Coffee

Can you imagine life before we could stop off and get our morning latte or espresso, that reviving treat that makes the journey to work or the school run so much easier to bear?

Before the arrival of Styrofoam or cardboard cups, coffees were confined to the café or coffee bar, but now they cheer up every occasion from sales meeting to PTA discussion. And who invented that miraculous plastic cover with the hole in it that means you can drink coffee on long and boring road trips? Many's the time I've been stuck in traffic, steam coming out of my ears in frustration, then sighted a Starbucks or Costa sign and calmed down to the point where I have accepted that traffic jams are just an annoying part of modern life.

Thank you, takeaway coffee-cup inventor, you have given me back my sanity.

Watching the Dawn Come Up

There is something incredibly life-enhancing about watching the day begin, no matter what season it is.

The first sign is a pink glow that tells you the sun is nearing the horizon and then miraculously it appears in the corner of the sky.

In a city, dawn is particularly wonderful because the sun reflects off tall buildings, lighting up their windows with gold and transforming even dull tower blocks into burnished palaces for just a few moments before they return to their businesslike greyness.

Having said that, the most glorious dawn I can ever remember seeing was in Turkey, when the moon was still in the sky.

Within half an hour the glory of the day is often over, but for that brief interlude the majesty of the universe is overwhelming.

Baking with Children

All our children loved baking cakes. It was the perfect activity – it taught them a skill and had its own built-in reward: eating the cake!

We had two books, *My First Baking Book* and *My First Cook Book*, both large-print easy-to-follow children's cookbooks which our children still occasionally refer to at the ages of 20, 18 and 13!

Little fairy cakes iced with sloppy pastel icing were always a favourite because they only took 15 minutes to bake and could be loaded down with silver balls, coloured sugar, hundreds and thousands, and even – if you wanted to go really over the top – sugar flowers.

Victoria sponge (my eldest daughter always used to call it 'scunge' which stuck, so for years it was 'Victoria scunge' in our household) was another favourite, though trickier, since it sometimes collapsed or failed to rise. One of our efforts was more like a large biscuit, but the children iced it all the same. Children are reassuringly unfussy about the quality of the end product.

My son often bakes peanut-butter cookies from the same book. Once, he even made them without the peanuts.

Even tiny children enjoy making cakes and I can't think of a nicer way of spending an hour than baking together, then sitting down with a cup of tea or coffee and consuming your own produce.

Cakes also make lovely, touching presents for people, especially for grannies and aunties and other doting-type adults. A tiny cake with the word 'Mum' written on it by small hands can literally bring tears to maternal eyes. I know – I was that mother!

Finding the Perfect Present

They always say one of the signs of growing up is that you discover the pleasure of giving as well as receiving, and there is definitely a special frisson in finding a gift that you just know someone will love.

Women are much better at (and also more stressed by) Christmas shopping because they really want the recipient of each gift to like it. Men tend to just want to get the whole thing over with, but women, with that famous female empathy, imagine how the recipient will feel on opening the present. This makes them prepared to spend far longer searching for it.

And when you do find something that's entirely right for a particular person, something you know they will appreciate, it's a pure delight.

One of my daughters recently passed an important English exam and I was looking for a cake to celebrate it. To my amazement I found a chocolate one with various decorations on top, one of which was a chocolate plaque of an Egyptian lady. I was instantly thrilled, knowing that my daughter had studied *Antony and Cleopatra* for the exam and how tickled she'd be at the coincidence.

It doubled my pleasure that it was so exactly right.

Hot-water Bottles

There is something irresistibly comforting about hot-water bottles. They are like being given a great big warm hug in bed. Some people prefer electric blankets, but the heat can be overwhelming. Hotties are perfect. They can just warm your feet, or that bit of your back that always seems to get coldest, and you can simply kick them out of the bed when you've reached maximum temperature.

They are also excellent if you and your partner happen to differ over ideal warmth levels, the sort of thing that could lead to a nasty difference of opinion were it not for your hottie friend.

The cosiest of all hot-water bottles are covered in fleece, so that you don't have to wrap them in towels as we did when I was growing up.

For an extra cuddle factor you can wrap your pyjamas or nightdress round the hottie just before you put them on – deliciously warm and a lot safer than one of my girlfriends' tip, gleaned from her granny, which was to pop your PJs into the oven before wearing them!

Making Stock

This is one men enjoy a lot, I've noticed.

And it's easy. Instead of throwing out the chicken carcass, chuck in an onion or two, a couple of carrots and some bouquet garni and fill it up with water.

The truth is, though, you may never use the stock once you've made it. Our freezer is full of stock my husband has made and never used!

Yet somehow the making of the stock seems as enjoyable as the using of it. This is to do with the way we want to live, the way we live in our imaginations. A stock pot simmering on the stove speaks of welcoming stews and homely fare, of childhood memories and a place that is warm and welcoming.

Of course if you do use the stock, even better. It makes truly fabulous risottos and soups. Plus you get the added pleasure of feeling you are reusing instead of wasting and that one meal can form the basis of the next in a way that must always have happened before the arrival of processed food and freezers.

So your risotto will be doubly satisfying.

Painting your Toenails

It's such a simple thing. And yet nail polish on the toes can transform feet from slightly ungainly things to objects of desirability and beauty in a matter of moments.

Unlike painting your fingernails, which can involve a lot of faffing about, cuticle-soaking, fake-nail creation and the attentions of a superior manicurist who looks at your hands as if you might confess to being a heavy lorry mechanic in your spare time, painting your toenails is different. For a start, you can do it yourself.

And apart from the occasional scrape on the bottom of a swimming pool, toenails chip much less than fingernails. When carefully decked out in red or pink they look perky, well cared-for and sexy. On nice tanned feet, painted toenails suggest the luscious allure of pomegranates or cherries. And painted with a dark purple like the famous Rouge Noir from Chanel that Uma Thurman wore in *Pulp Fiction*, they suggest erotic possibilities.

Even Cleopatra knew the appeal of a painted toenail – though hers were tinted with henna or gum Arabic rather than non-chip acrylic.

Seeing your Luggage Appear at Airports

Contrary to all our fantasies, holidays aren't always filled with hedonistic pleasure – they can actually be pretty stressful.

First there's finding somewhere you all want to go to, and with families containing teenagers as well as parents, that's quite a challenge. Then you hope the place actually looks like the brochure and that your own particular room doesn't overlook the car park. If it's a villa you hope it isn't damp, dark or infested with scorpions (this happened to a family I know who went to Tuscany). You hope the swimming pool isn't filled with algae and that your teenagers aren't (too) filled with cheap cocktails.

But one simple pleasure is just the lovely relief when you arrive at the airport and your luggage arrives there too. Pretty basic, you might think, but enough people have experienced starting a holiday without their suitcase to make it a straightforward joy when the clothes they brought with them come rumbling round on the airport carousel.

Plenty can still go wrong, but at least they'll be wearing the right clothes when it does.

Triumphing over Technology

Technology is wonderful. Liberating. Enabling. It opens doors to the world. But it can also be infuriating and unfathomable, leaving you with a sense of helpless fury, feeling both bewildered and inept.

Some of this is to do with age. Children are now called 'digital natives', while the rest of are us 'digital immigrants' groping our way round technology in the dark, condemned to hours trying to get through to distant helpdesks.

I was once sent a birthday card which featured a woman trying to set a video recorder. She was turning to her six-month-old baby, asking, 'And how do I set the recording time?' A bit outdated now, but we all know the feeling. Even my teenagers sometimes feel technology is outstripping them.

So my triumph was particularly sweet the other day when

I mended my own printer. I had been advised by all and sundry to chuck it out. No one mends technology, you know, you just replace it.

And I mended it myself!

This was satisfying on a number of levels: a) I felt I was defeating the advance of a cut-throat capitalism which counsels replacing rather fixing anything; b) I saved lots of money; c) I greatly enjoyed telling my husband I'd done it.

White T-shirts

Now and then an item comes along that's so iconic and simple it works on every occasion and lasts forever, irrespective of fashion.

The white T-shirt is one of them. It appears everywhere and in all guises, at all price levels. Some people even spend their lives looking for the perfect model.

The white T-shirt is simple, sexy, fresh and timeless. It's a true classic. It probably looks best with blue jeans – two classics together.

Fashion designers try and improve on it with velvet or fancy edging.

Forget it. The white T-shirt is perfect just as it is.

Sticking Up a Slogan

Advertisers and motivational speakers understand the power of the slogan. It's the pithy sentence that sums up a complicated thought. Something that gets to you emotionally and inspires you to action, whether it's drinking Coke or changing the planet.

Provided they mean something to you personally, slogans can be very useful in reminding you of something you've undertaken to do – breaking a bad habit perhaps or being more embracing about life.

The slogan I've got on my own wall (because I tend to be a glass half-empty type unless I watch myself) is from Omar Khayyam. It says:

> *Be Happy for This Moment.*
> *This Moment is Your Life.*

That's something that I quite often need to remind myself of in the everydayness and annoyance of daily life.

Sleeping in a Four-poster Bed

I'm not sure why this is one of life's Great Romantic Experiences, but it is.

Perhaps it's the sense of history, or the idea of King Charles II and his mistress Nell Gwynne romping in one, but there's something about the four-poster that is incredibly sexy and alluring.

Hotels know they can charge extra for their four-poster rooms and that they always go first, often to honeymooning couples. In England there are even a few hotels that claim Queen Elizabeth I slept in theirs. That's unlikely, unfortunately, and would probably have been pretty uncomfortable, as Elizabethans always liked their beds to face north, so they were often freezing cold!

Perhaps the idea of sleeping in such a romantic bed unleashes all our wildest (and deeply unPC) fantasies of being ravished by ruthless rakes or wicked pirates, but everyone should try and sleep in a four-poster at least once in their life – even if Johnny Depp isn't available to accompany them.

Choosing a Perfume

We all nurture that fantasy of finding a 'signature' perfume, a scent that evokes our own individual complex personality so well that people instantly know when we've been in a room.

For most of that's what it remains – a fantasy. Unless you happen to be J-Lo, or Elizabeth Taylor, or even Britney Spears, you probably won't have your very own perfume.

How boring anyway to use just one scent when you can have 10 that match your mood or personality or life stage. When I was a teenager I owned one called Pagan, whose selling line was 'Don't wear it if you're only teasing'. The implication was that it would drive men so wild with desire they wouldn't be able to control themselves. My convent girlfriends and I bought vats of it.

Quite often when you can smell someone's perfume in adult life it's because it's one of those musk-laden ones that hit you over the head – or because they're wearing too much of it.

Like a lot of women I get bored with a perfume after a while and rarely finish a whole bottle. I chose my current one because six rather sexy men nominated it in a magazine as one they'd like to wake up next to.

Ah, the deluding yet wonderful power of the atomizer!

Putting Photos in an Album

Some people store their photos on their computer, or show them to their friends via the TV, or send them to their mates via file-sharing. Others forget them and leave them in their cameras, but there's still nothing like the fun of making an album.

Modern albums have pockets to slip the photos in (none of those annoying little sticky holder things that are supposed to hold your photos in place and never do). They even have space for you to write a little description of when and where by the side.

I try to do one of our family holiday as soon as possible when we get home and often get them off the shelf to look at. They always bring back happy memories. Last year I got ambitious and planned a collage involving shells and things I'd found on the beach. Needless to say, I'm no artist and it never got made.

Albums are simple and still the most user-friendly way of recording your memories. And they have a solidity, a permanence, that means you won't wipe or lose them.

When each of my family members and I became adults my mother made an album for each of us and mine has proved incredibly precious. As I became a journalist and novelist in later life (something my mother didn't live to see, sadly), I found myself referring to my album more and more.

With my own children I have gone a step further and made them all a series of books in which I've stuck scraps of paper, school reports, cards and letters they've sent me, programmes of concerts or plays they've taken part in, certificates, drawings and even odd and funny little notes they've sent to each other. Somehow these capture their individual personalities in a different way from photos and they love reading them!

Small Routines

Humans are creatures of habit.

I once read an article that said you should change your side of the bed every five years to stop your marriage getting too boring. What would you do with all that stuff you keep by the bedside?

Routines – even the annoying ones – are what give life its shape. No matter how busy I am I always feel happiest and most in control if I get a washing load on and pack the dishwasher before I start work. On a really good day I will also have decided what is for supper and walked the dog – though that rarely happens!

There are other routines that have become like breathing: sorting out the recycling, emptying bins, reading the newspaper, picking up damp towels from the floor, turning on the computer, answering e-mails.

These routines are often quite annoying, yet I know that when I feel down or isolated they will absorb me enough to get me going. Such is the framework on which our lives are built.

And, curiously, some of my routines seem to be inherited. I used to get annoyed at my mother for plumping up the cushions on the sofa before going to bed, but now I do it too. Then I saw it as a signal of suburban fussiness; now it seems a practical way of making the room look its best. In turn, it drives my children mad.

Perhaps life is a journey from exhilarating spontaneity to reassuring predictability.

You are, as they say, what you do.

Reading Poetry

There are moments in life when only poetry will do.

At times of great emotion it's often to poetry that we turn rather than to fiction or to films to understand the heights and depths of what is happening to us. And the two poetic themes we seek out tend to be Love and Death.

When you are ecstatically in love, requitedly or not, then only Shakespeare or Byron or Elizabeth Barrett Browning seem to understand what you're talking about.

And when someone you love dies, the only answer seems to be in verse from Dylan Thomas or W. H. Auden or John Donne.

Poetry is the quintessence of emotion, and when pain or grief or joy wrenches us out of the everyday we need poets to do the speaking for us.

Hanging on to a Parking Space

This isn't a very nice confession, but I take particular pleasure in telling someone who wants my parking space that sorry, I'm staying in it. Actually I'm not at all sorry I'm staying in it. I hate people who want my space so much that sometimes I tell them I'm staying even when I'm not.

Then I take mean and unedifying delight in watching them drive off.

For a few seconds I sit there, luxuriating in the possession of my precious parking space before owning up to the fact that I didn't need it at all.

Pathetic? Childish? Self-centred? Yes, all of the above. But curiously and wickedly pleasurable all the same.

Stargazing

If you ever feel (don't we all?) that your own little problems are getting on top of you, go stargazing. There's something about the grandeur of the night sky and the infinity of the stars that makes you feel both peaceful and full of wonder.

To really appreciate a starry, starry night, head away from the city, because the bleed of streetlight dims the extraordinary clarity of the starscape. At our small cottage in the English countryside I climb to the top of a hill and just lie back and gaze until I almost feel in a trance.

It takes 15 minutes for your iris to open up fully, so you need to be patient and wrap up.

If the night is clear and cold and there's no moon, you can see thousands of stars and it doesn't take much knowledge to spot the Plough, the Great Bear and the Pole Star and even the distant galaxy of Andromeda.

Even if you can't tell your Orion from your Ursa Major, the sheer enormity and brightness of the sky will make you feel that the universe is a pretty amazing place. And there's nothing like being outside at night to feel that even in a world overcrowded with millions of people, you can occasionally have the planet to yourself!

Airports

It may be a bit of a cliché, but I adore airports and always find them life-enhancing, even when I'm just meeting someone and not going anywhere myself. They are so full of drama and feeling and hope.

Sometimes whole families turn up to meet flights from the Indian subcontinent, bright in silks and loaded with bunches of flowers. Then some tiny old lady appears, looking baffled and anxious, and is scooped up into a crowd of laughing relatives.

Then there are the lovers ready to pull each other into a passionate clinch, oblivious of the crowds all around them. Once I saw a boy with a box of chocolates and an enormous teddy bear waiting for a girl who looked absolutely horrified when she saw it. Your heart went out to him.

Then there are mothers waiting for fathers coming home from a business trip, children all neatly dressed, and fathers waiting for mothers, with the children looking a mess in party dresses and the wrong socks.

Airports have everything – happy reunions and tearful departures – and if you look around you when you're there, you'll find all the drama of a soap opera, only it just happens to be real life!

Seeing Life as a Web, Not a Ladder

I was very struck, years ago, to hear a psychologist describe the different attitudes men and women had to life and what gave them both satisfaction.

Men, the psychologist asserted, tended to see life as a ladder. The task of being male seemed to involve starting at the bottom and climbing to the top.

Women, on the other hand, saw life more as a web. Their sense of achievement was made up of an intricate pattern of small satisfactions which threaded outwards, encompassing family, friendships, work and domesticity, as well as a sense of place and meaning in the world.

I have found this concept a useful tool in understanding what does and does not bring me lasting satisfaction. It has made me stand back from the most obvious ways of measuring life – money, success, approval – and view things with a cooler eye, asking myself, 'What really makes me happy?'

And, like the spider, it seems to be spinning my web as wide as I can and recognizing that small pleasures and rituals are often as reliable a source of happiness as big important ones.

Wrapping Presents

Wrapping presents isn't always one of life's great pleasures. At Christmas it can be an exhausting chore that always seems to be done at midnight on Christmas Eve. But at other times, when you are wrapping for a friend or a child and imagining their face when they open it, present-wrapping is indeed a delightful activity.

Maybe it's because in modern life we're all running to stand still and our creativity doesn't get that many outlets. But gift-wrapping is rather magical in itself. It transforms an essential activity into something special.

The only problem with it is that if you get too carried away, the wrapping can be more special than the present – a sure way of inducing disappointment in the recipient.

Taking Something Back to a Shop

A complicated pleasure, this, but one a lot of us confess to.

The object of shopping is to find something you want and enjoy owning it. Yet there is also a perverse pleasure in seeing if you like something, deciding that you either don't want or don't need it and then taking it back. The refunding of your money makes you feel that you've had the pleasure of buying something without the pain of paying for it.

At its most extreme this process has been labelled 'shopping bulimia' and is apparently an increasing problem to traders.

But used occasionally it's a perfectly healthy, and even enjoyable, way of feeling that capitalism doesn't completely have you in its grip. It's a small and quite rewarding stand against the system.

Ripe Peaches

This is a pleasure that can only be pursued on holiday. You just don't get ripe peaches in many countries, certainly not in the UK, where I live. Here peaches are often sold hard and apple-like with the advice that they should 'ripen at home' on a sunny windowsill, but most often they go off before they ever become ripe at all.

But Mediterranean peaches! That's a different story. Large and downy and red-yellowy, just beginning to go soft, smelling of sunshine and fruitiness, with a glorious intensity of flavour… Not to mention the juice that always runs down your chin and splashes onto your clean T-shirt.

I can still taste the peaches I ate in the South of France on holiday as a child and each year I hope to find them again. Like Proust's Madeleines, the mere scent of them transports me to a beach on the Riviera.

For the peach purist, the outer skin needs to be removed. Not for me. I wash them and gobble them whole, realizing with each glorious mouthful that I won't taste anything like that for another year. Until next summer. And the next perfect peach.

Appreciating the Past

When you're a teenager it's easy to believe that only the present matters. History is something you learn at school and forget as soon as possible.

But the past is all around us, making sense of the present, of who we are.

People often say they wish they'd talked properly to their grandparents. Instead they saw them as old people and didn't realize how interesting their lives might have been. And that they carried part of them in themselves.

There is a wonderful poem by Philip Larkin called 'An Arundel Tomb', where he meditates on the stone effigies of a medieval earl and countess who, perhaps by some quirk of the sculptor's, are holding hands. This somehow makes them seem modern and meaningful to us, and in love, though perhaps this is just a lie that we want to believe.

All the same, that gesture cuts across 500 years and

brings the past right into the present. We *want* it to signify love, and the thought gives us a sense of connection to previous generations that is both vivid and moving.

Having a sense of the past makes life in the present immeasurably richer.

Gossiping

I firmly believe that behaving badly now and then can be good for you. And one of the easiest and cheapest ways to behave badly is gossiping.

We know we shouldn't. We know that gossip probably consists of things that should remain private. *But still*, the joy of being the first in possession of some exciting information or of being able to impart someone else's bad news!

That wonderful German word *Schadenfreude* says it all: pleasure in the misfortunes of others.

Yes – gossip isn't really gossip unless there's a shred of malice in it. I know this won't suit the elevated spiritual principles of some, but there it is.

Lighting Candles

Candles are one of those miracle mood-lifters. When I was a child I went to a convent boarding school and can still remember its wonderfully evocative scents: incense, floor polish and the beeswax of the candles that filled the church.

Candles have come a long way since then. Now so many of them have delicious aromas that have little to do with bees. Each is able to create a different mood. Vanilla is a lovely one to light while you're in the bath – maybe a whole row of them plus tealights – in your own little luxurious ritual. My favourite is bluebell. A good-quality one gives you the illusion of taking a bath in the middle of a bluebell wood!

At Christmas it's a must in our home to light spice candles, which fill the house with the rich and evocative scents of orange, lemon, cinnamon, cloves and nutmeg, and instantly transport me back to the delights of childhood Christmases.

But even adding a plain unscented candle to the supper

table can raise the meal from your usual Friday night roast chicken to an occasion with style and a bit of pizzazz.

I once experimented with putting three different-coloured candles in our ancient candelabra and they looked great in a wacky Bohemian way.

When I worked in television we made a short film about a woman who was famous for giving Tuscan dinner parties, spreading the table with strands of ivy, tiered plates of bluish-purple damsons and blue-black figs, the whole effect complemented by grape-coloured candles. It looked stunning. I've never had the nerve (or risked the accusation of pretentiousness) to copy it, but I've always wanted to!

But even a simple white candle makes an ordinary meal special and reminds us that meals are about more than just food. They are occasions to be savoured.

Finding Money

The silly thing is that finding money cheers you up even when it's your own money in the first place.

My whole day is brightened when I delve into the pocket of an old coat and discover a crumpled note. Money down the back of sofas, hidden under car seats, in the make-up pouch of rarely used handbags – finding it is always pure pleasure.

The same applies when you find that you have more than you thought in your bank account or get a rebate from the taxman. But it's not the pure unalloyed joy of finding an actual real valid banknote you can go straight out and spend. That feels as though someone has given you an unexpected present.

You have a duty to go out and spend it on yourself right now.

Making a Fire

There are some tasks that, even though they are small or routine, are vast in the pleasure they give. Making a fire is one of these. Perhaps it's an unacknowledged link with our Neanderthal past, when we were in a life-or-death struggle against the elements, but making a fire can fill you with an enormous sense of wellbeing. Whether you use a dozen firelighters to get it going or are the boy-scout type who just uses a single match, the satisfaction of watching the flames begin to flicker is immense.

My mother-in-law used to make her own kindling by plaiting old newspapers into fat tapers that helped to start the whole blaze off, and she always said it was one of her favourite tasks. I have shown my son how to do the same and now it is his special job. Already he shares that sense of amazing achievement when the fire catches.

There's even a special pleasure in getting the right blend of kindling, coal and wood that's neither so damp that it spits and fills the room with smoke nor so dry that it burns through in a moment.

By the side of our fire we have a copy of an old woodman's poem to remind us that though we live in the twenty-first century, these are age-old concerns:

Oak logs will warm you well
If they are old and dry.
Larch logs and Pinewood smell
But sparks will fly.

Ash logs, all smooth and grey,
Burn them green or old.
Buy up all that come your way,
They're worth their weight in gold.

Pretending to Be a Tourist

Sometimes we spend large sums of money visiting other cities and forget the pleasures of the place where we actually live ourselves. From time to time I play a little game which is great fun and can make you see your home town through new eyes: I pretend to be a tourist.

By this I don't mean I put on a fake French accent and start asking people for directions, but try to see the city I live in as if I were a visitor. I ask myself what I'd do if I were only here for a weekend. Which landmarks would I go and look at? Which museums? Would I take time out to sit in pavement cafés? Take a river trip?

Once, when looking for Christmas cards, I suddenly caught sight of Trafalgar Square with its Christmas tree all lit up and realized how many times I'd passed by without noticing the magic, yet I was always saying I wanted to go Christmas shopping in New York. That day London took my breath away in its wintry beauty.

You don't have to be a tourist in a capital city, of course, or a city at all. The point is to look at the familiar with new eyes.

Try it – it really works.

Roasted Vegetables

Now and then a culinary fashion comes along that is so simple, so delicious and so useful that you can't imagine life without it.

Pasta is one. My children can't believe that when I was growing up we rarely ate pasta. In my childhood everything came with potatoes. Being Irish by background, the potato was our staple food. When I told my children this they imagined Irish people sitting under trees eating potatoes for every meal. Not quite, but we ate an awful lot of them.

I first encountered a roasted red pepper at a barbecue about 10 years ago. It was charred on the outside and sweet in the middle and it instantly took the humble barbecue food that accompanied it to delicious and exotic heights.

Since then I have roasted vegetables as often as possible: courgettes, aubergines, tomatoes on the vine, peppers of all colours, asparagus, butternut squash, French beans…

They look and taste delicious, and in 15 minutes, just like that barbecued pepper, they turn a simple meal into a colourful tempting feast.

If you don't use too much oil and keep them relatively crunchy, they're even good for you.

A Perfectly Made Bed

At my convent boarding school we were taught how to do 'hospital corners', a method by which flat sheets were tightly stretched over the bed and held in position by a deft tucking movement. Our beds were even inspected by the nuns.

Hospital corners have all but disappeared with the arrival of that wonderful invention, the fitted sheet. (Except that they're hell to iron – life always has a way of making you pay!) The widespread use of duvet covers has also revolutionized the bed-making process and made it incredibly easy. (Tell that to my teenagers.)

Yet there is still an art to making a bed enticing. Clean sheets (still an object of desire to most of us), beautifully smoothed out, are essential, as are plumped-up pillows, fat as large hens and quite often padded with their feathers. The finishing touches come with toned cushions and artfully arranged quilts or comforters.

The only trouble with beautifully made beds is resisting the desire to climb back in as soon as you've made them.

Scrunchy Hair Ties

It would be difficult to explain to a man, and perhaps a woman with extremely short hair, the miracle of design that is the scrunchy hair tie. Nevertheless, miracle it is.

For any men reading (and for the editors of various dictionaries and spellchecks in which this important word does not feature), a scrunchy is a piece of elastic covered in fabric used by many women to keep their hair from falling over their face or inadvertently getting wet in the bath or shower. It is one of the most useful inventions known to woman.

Before the arrival of the scrunchy, women were obliged to tie their hair up with ponytail ties fitted with nasty brass closures that were agony to remove because your hair caught in them, or actual rubber bands designed for putting round jam jars, or even, in the case of the heroine of one of my novels, leopardskin bikini briefs.

Then along came the scrunchy. This admirable object managed to tie your hair back and occasionally look quite nice without even making a nasty ridge on your hairstyle like the old sort did.

School uniform manufacturers have even started making scrunchies to match schoolgirls' cotton frocks and I noticed the other day that the team I follow has started to offer a red-and-white one in the colours of Arsenal Football Club.

So this humble yet irreplaceable device is destined for a long and happy future.

Spa Days

Spas – which used to be rather curiously referred to as 'health farms' – were once the prerogative of the very rich. The rest of us could only read about them in gossip columns and glossy magazines. But since that marvellous invention, the spa day, came along, spas are a possibility for most of us – if only for a birthday treat.

Spa days have become a big favourite for hen parties before a wedding. The bride and her closest friends go on them to chat and be cosseted, swapping jokes and delicious gossip while wrapped in huge fluffy towels.

Lots of mothers and daughters go too. I took my two daughters after they'd had a gruelling period of exams and, though I'm not much of a beauty-parlour devotee, really enjoyed the feeling of being 'out of time'. I loved the peace and the pampering, but rather drew the line at the almost mystical atmosphere some spas aim for. Whale music is fine, but when the beautician put on a CD of monks chanting plainsong I felt distinctly uncomfortable – maybe because I was educated by nuns!

Sometimes it feels as though beauty and fitness *are* the new religion, but that doesn't mean a spa day isn't a huge treat, especially if you take the whole thing for what it is – a delightful pleasure rather than a way of life!

Appreciating the Ordinary

The poet Pablo Neruda wrote an ode to a pair of his socks.

Maybe they were wonderful socks, warm yet breathable, just the right length. Maybe wearing them brought back memories of places he had walked to in them or the woman he had been with when he put them on.

An appreciation of the ordinary things in life is one of the best gifts we can be given because ordinary things are always there for us.

The perfect green circle of a slice of courgette, the spicy tang of mulled wine, forks laid neatly embracing each other in a drawer, lovely italic handwriting on a letter – when you look around, you find that every day is filled with small objects of beauty and order.

All we have to do is notice them.

Being Ill

I'm not talking real illness here, obviously. Nothing chronic or life-threatening or even – let's face it – uncomfortable or painful. If you're really ill, even with 'flu, you turn out the lights, pull up the covers and sleep.

No, I'm talking bit of a temperature, slightly sore throat, fairly exhausted and sorry for yourself sort of ill. This illness benefits greatly from somebody spoiling you and bringing you little meals of the boiled egg variety and glasses of lemon barley water.

It's the kind of illness men are particularly good at (often driving women mad).

With this kind of illness, sympathy is better medicine than paracetamol. It usually only lasts about a day (one of its defining characteristics) before the sufferer gets bored. In my view it should be indulged, both in oneself and others. It's the body's way of saying 'I need a rest. And someone to show me they love me.' Even your dog will do, in this department. Though dogs, sadly, are not very good at making cups of tea.

I once read a wonderful definition of being married which insisted that in a good marriage you could take it in turns to feel pathetic. Needing a day's illness comes under that heading. That's why it should be indulged. And reciprocated.

Comforting Casseroles

Casseroles are the opposite of fast food. You prepare the ingredients, put them in the oven to cook slowly and then forget about them. Sometimes literally. But casseroles are like wise old people who've seen a thing or two. They are kind and tolerant. They don't mind being forgotten, sometimes for hours on end. Providing they don't run out of liquid, they will stew quietly away and just get better.

They can also be eaten in a user-friendly way, expanding to meet unexpected guests or being raided by starving teenagers before they go out. Our dog also very much enjoys the leftovers, carrots and all, though rarely gets them, because casseroles are even better the next day. Accompanied by a crisp-skinned baked potato, they make the perfect leftover lunch.

Casseroles are a little out of fashion now, pushed into the background by fussy techniques that have to be done at the last minute. But they will stand the test of time. When winter comes, what could be nicer and more welcoming than a rich boeuf Bourguignon, or carbonnade in its layer of mustard-soaked baguette, or a lamb hotpot covered in thin slices of crisp potato?

And a casserole doesn't even need a yelling and swearing chef to serve it.

Learning to Accept a Compliment

The funny thing is, we all make an effort. We go to the hairdresser's, buy new clothes, wear make-up. And then when someone tells us we look pretty or sexy or chic, we get embarrassed. We start mumbling, 'I've just had my hair done,' or, 'I usually look a mess,' or even question the motives of whoever is paying us the compliment.

When all we really need to do is say 'Thank you.'

Sharpening Pencils

This is another of those tasks that works on two levels of enjoyment.

The first level is that sharpening pencils is a pleasurable activity in itself, provided you have a good pencil sharpener. Personally I favour the small ones made of chrome or steel, not the fancy wall-mounted kind. We were given one of these fancy sharpeners as a gift and it never seemed to work, even though the person who gave it to us swore by them.

Once you have your sharpener, sit at a table with a piece of kitchen towel to catch your shavings and get sharpening!

This is one of those jobs I did before each school term because that's when my kids wanted to throw away all their pencils and crayons and get new ones, irrespective of whether last term's were any good. Usually I managed to rescue at least half and restore them, perfectly sharpened, to the respective pencil cases. Occasionally a crayon broke and buggered up the sharpener and I had to dig it out with my good tweezers, but largely this was a calming, enjoyable process.

And the other level? Newly sharpened pencils are like a blank calendar. They are a new start, a fresh beginning. They mean anything could happen. Anything is possible when you are holding a sharp HB pencil.

The Blue of a Swimming Pool

No wonder David Hockney loved painting that very special blue of a Los Angeles swimming pool.

Swimming pool blue is a complex colour. Alluring and inviting, yet also redolent of success and aspiration and privilege.

Most of us only get to have our own pools in a rented holiday villa or hotel. So swimming-pool blue is all about exclusivity and joining the élite club of the pool owner.

Fortunately children don't understand this. Like rock stars who drive cars into them, kids just think swimming pools are about having fun and all they want to do is dive-bomb into them and soak their host with chlorine-drenched water.

Which is probably very good for them.

A Pot of Basil

There is nothing on earth as evocative as breathing in the scent of basil. When you tear it roughly between your fingers it instantly releases a pungent aroma that transports you to the warmth of the Mediterranean or the blue-green hills of Tuscany.

In fact there is nothing like the delicious simplicity of a tomato and mozzarella salad with fresh basil sprinkled on it. And the beauty of it is that most supermarkets now sell pots and vacuum-packs of basil, thyme, marjoram and coriander.

Even more rewarding is growing your own herbs. Sprinkling rosemary from your own garden or window box over lamb, your own thyme over roasted new potatoes or your own mint into a barbecue marinade completely transforms your attitude to the food. Maybe it's because we feel suddenly in touch with our hunter-gatherer selves, but the pleasure this gives is overwhelming.

Rosemary and mint both grow almost like weeds once you've planted them, but if you don't have the time or the space to grow your own, you can get almost as much enjoyment out of buying them. Sprinkling fresh herbs onto your cooking will still make you feel as though you have your very own link with the cycle of nature.

Birthday Breakfasts

When I was a kid my birthday was the one day when I was able to choose what I wanted for breakfast: Coca-Cola and cake.

Starting your birthday with a bang is vital, it seems to me. After all, it might be a school day or a work day and breakfast might be the best moment. So we've evolved a family ritual where everyone gets their presents and cards, plus birthday cake, at breakfast time. If it's a weekend we often have breakfast in bed. It all feels wonderfully naughty and decadent. But it does ensure that every birthday starts off special, even if they go downhill after that.

Cutting Your Toenails

OK, I know this sounds seriously weird, but there is pleasure to be had in cutting your toenails.

Somehow managing to achieve that satisfying straight line across the top – as well as resisting (or sometimes giving in to) the temptation to cut down the sides where the chiropodist says you mustn't – is an extremely rewarding experience. Maybe it's a throwback to ancient humanity; I don't know. But I do know it is one of life's unexpected – and untalked-about – little pleasures.

Implements are important. Men favour nail clippers; women go for scissors. And there is one vital piece of advice, especially if you want to stay attached to your partner: *Don't do it in front of them!*

Getting Outdoors

We are meant to take 10,000 steps a day and most of us take about a third of those. And yet taking some kind of exercise is reckoned by psychologists to be the best therapy for depression – far better than Prozac, for instance.

And if the exercise you take isn't in a gym (these always remind me of the 'Satanic mills' William Blake describes, even though they are brightly lit rather than dark) but in the great outdoors, it's good for the soul too.

Studies have shown that being close to nature is good for us. Patients in America were found to recover more quickly even if they could just *see* trees from their hospital beds.

There's a regular walk I do along a riverbank in the English countryside and it's no exaggeration to say that each time I do it, I see something new. And even though the walk is probably no more than half-an-hour long, I always come back feeling that life is good, no matter how glum I was when I began it.

It may be a cliché that nature heals the troubled mind, but it's true.

Linen Napkins

Maybe it's how clean and fresh and starched they look, but there's nothing quite like newly laundered napkins, especially against a white tablecloth.

Paper napkins are very pretty too, and far more practical, but they just don't look the same.

Linen napkins, with their touch of impractical luxury, decree that it's a special occasion.

I love the look of plain white, but for utter perfection, pale blue napkins are more original and pale pink the loveliest of all.

Of course washing and ironing them is a fag, but somehow, even if you only use them for very special occasions, it's worth the effort for the pleasure you get from seeing them, crisply inviting, summoning you to a little old-fashioned luxury.

Singing Along to Musicals

Go on, confess. You've done it, haven't you? You've joined the reverend mother singing 'How Do You Solve a Problem Like Maria?' or sympathized with 'Officer Krupky' in *West Side Story* or tried to remember how to spell 'supercalifragilisticexpialidocious'. We all have.

One of life's great pleasures is finding that you know the words to all the great musicals without apparently ever having learned them. In fact the sign of a really great musical is that the songs embed themselves effortlessly in your consciousness.

My husband once serenaded me with 'Thank Heaven for Leetle Girls' at 5 a.m. one morning when I was going off filming in France. I'm not sure how impressed I was, except with the fact that he remembered every single word!

And there's nothing better to make a long journey pass pleasantly than to sing along with every song from *The Sound of Music* or *Grease*. Even terrible singers can lose themselves in the chorus of 'I Enjoy Being a Girl'. And it's a lot more fun than everyone being plugged into their own individual iPods.

The Smell of Petrol

This may sound strange, but it's amazing how many people love the smell of petrol.

It's also one of those pungent aromas that drag you straight back in time - like mothballs, mint on new potatoes, wood smoke in autumn, fresh laundry, Love Hearts, lavender bags or the sharp clean smell of pine needles.

All of us carry around our own personal library of scents which have an incredibly powerful and immediate effect on us because they bypass the conscious mind. Fortunately most of mine are comforting and nostalgically pleasant. Except for the smell of spinach. That takes me back to my convent boarding school. The smell of the spinach served up there was one of the most repulsive on earth. Even Popeye would have been turned off by it.

It took serious re-education by one of my daughters, who is a great cook, to persuade me that spinach lightly wilted in butter could be a million miles from the smelly evil green slop we were given at school.

But one whiff and I'd be back there, shovelling the stuff into the pocket of my school skirt.

Being Extravagant

I realize that many of the small pleasures I've evoked are about saving, mending, restoring and reusing because these are highly satisfying things to do in a world that seems so driven by consumerism. But that's no reason to stop yourself being extravagant now and then.

When I got married a few years ago to the man I had been living with for 20 years, I bought a wildly expensive handbag made by Lulu Guinness. It looked like a black velvet flowerpot with a red rose attached to the top and was probably the most expensive and the least useful object I had ever bought in my life. You could only fit a lipstick in it! Even my small mobile didn't fit in, nor a wallet nor a comb.

But how I longed for it!

I have probably used it all of twice, but I don't regret the extravagance. In fact the extravagance was probably part of the pleasure, marking it out from the usual and everyday.

It remains my mad, crazy, over-the-top wedding indulgence.

And who knows, maybe it'll be an antique of the future?

Chocolate

Ambrosia isn't the food of the gods; chocolate is.

I am not at all surprised that the Aztecs used it in religious ceremonies. It has also been branded as 'food of the devil' – maybe because it leads to lax sofa-lying and maximum self-indulgence.

Slim French housewives recommend eating one square of extra-dark chocolate every day – which shows that French housewives are not chocoholics. The true chocoholic cannot stop at one square. Even stopping at one box can be a challenge. And shamingly I have to confess to eating one of my children's Easter eggs – but only because they already had about 10 each!

Scientists currently believe that the reason chocolate is so addictive is that it triggers the release of endorphins, which produce a warm inner glow. Unfortunately this warm inner glow tends only to last until the next chocolate bar, but it helps explain why we turn to chocolate when we're lonely or depressed.

It seems to me that chocolate is unique in the intensity of the pleasure it produces. I can't think of a single other food which feels as orgasmic as chocolate (though good ice cream, mature Cheddar cheese and crusty new bread all have their moments).

I hate all those killjoys who come up with sayings like 'A moment on your lips, a lifetime on your hips'. Instead I proudly display the message on the cushion given to me by a friend who understood my true nature:

*Just hand over the chocolate and
no one will get hurt.*

Folding Washing Instead of Ironing It

Surveys occasionally throw out the news that some people love ironing. Personally I hate it, and apart from ironing linen garments and the odd smart shirt, I have dedicated myself to finding ways to avoid it.

My cousin showed me how, if you hang blouses and shirts on coat hangers, they dry crease-free, and I have evolved a nifty way of folding everything else rather as they do on the shelves in Gap, which produces passably smooth T-shirts, jeans and trousers.

One friend confessed to actually ironing her knickers. I told her I thought she should see someone.

I don't want to be intolerant here. Each to their own way of surviving the rigours of domestic life. My friend insisted she found it relaxing.

But on the whole I'd rather be sitting on the sofa with my feet up.

Giving Blood

I have rarely found an activity that gives you back so much for so little effort.

This seems to work on a number of levels:

- It makes you think. The whole act of giving blood reminds you of the arbitrary nature of life, how lucky you are to be alive and healthy, how different things could be and indeed are for a lot of people. This is useful in itself.

- It makes you feel good that you are helping. If you're like me, it may have taken you a while to get round to doing it. You had it on your 'Things to Do' list and now you've finally done it. And it might save someone's life.

- It's fun. All right, not if you can't bear needles. But the atmosphere in the centres where people go to give blood is life-enhancing in itself. You'll find all types of people there: big beefy guys who're quite scared of admitting they're nervous, chatty old men who give blood all the time because it gets them out of the house, working women in a hurry and, the last time I went, a stunningly beautiful girl wearing a micro-skirt and the most amazing four-inch heels made of bronze calf-leather. She looked like an upmarket lap-dancer and there she was giving blood!

- And you get a drink and biscuits and a little lie-down afterwards.

- You also get told your blood group, which is useful information to know. Mine is B positive. I decided that was a message from the gods and have adopted 'Be Positive' as my new mantra!

Rediscovering Your Instincts

It's a curious phenomenon of modern life that so many of us have lost touch with our instincts. We read books, we follow trends, but we rarely listen to what our own inner voice tells us.

From the moment our babies are born we don't know how to treat them without help from experts. The same is true when we want to change our own lives – we turn to life coaches, motivational gurus or agony aunts. Perhaps it's because our lives are no longer governed by hunger and need, or by the seasons. No pattern is imposed on them by light and darkness. These once dictated the working hours in the day, but now everything is down to choice – what we do, where we live, whom we live with – and that makes us so scared that our inner promptings recede to the point where we can't hear them any more.

And yet when we do trust our instincts – recognizing that a situation might be dangerous and avoiding it, for instance, working out for ourselves when a child is old enough to go out alone, making up our minds about people's characters – we are often right.

One of my daughters, when aged three, got a rubber stuck up her nose. I panicked and wanted to call in the experts. But her 18-year-old carer calmly put her finger over her nose and made her blow. Out came the rubber. I, the supposedly successful, sophisticated mother, had completely lost touch with my instincts. This calm and sensible 18-year-old had not. Thank heavens.

It's a lesson I have often thought about since and I have tried to be more instinctive. I'm sure we often instinctively know the answers we seek. But we somehow need someone else to tell us.

Telling Yourself You're Wonderful

Like most busy women I have an endless 'Things to Do' list. And although having a list like that can be quite satisfying when you tick the items off, it also builds in a sense of failure if you don't get through it.

The other day I was scurrying round trying to do three things at once and I started feeling that sense of internal rushing, rather like a big wave approaching and dragging you down with it. Suddenly I stopped and had to mentally take myself aside. 'Look,' I told myself sternly, 'you've been to the supermarket, bought dog food and picked up that new washbasin. And it's only 9.30! Most people aren't even at work yet! You should remind yourself how amazing you are!'

So I did.

And I recommend that you do it too the next time you get that sinking feeling that life is running away with you.

Say: 'Actually, I'm pretty damn amazing!'

Because, let's face it, you are.

Writing a Thank-you Note

We do so much by e-mail now that actually putting pen to paper has more meaning than ever.

You have to stop a moment. You have to think. You have to try and say something genuine.

And receiving a thank-you note – especially one that sounds genuine – is an exceptionally nice experience. And if it sounds fake at least you can admire the technique!

Candlelit Baths

Men, I have discovered, enjoy these just as much as women.

Perhaps we all harbour the fantasy of a Balinese extravaganza featuring a tub filled with flowers.

The nearest most of us can get to that (especially on a weekly basis) is to lock the doors, light some scented candles and retreat from the stress of modern living.

Gorgeous.

Decorating a Christmas Tree

Of all the Christmas rituals, this is the one I enjoy most.

We always have a fight about when to buy the tree. It's a tricky question because children want Christmas to start as early as possible and grown-ups prefer to delay the whole thing until nearer the big day. My mother never allowed us to have the tree until Christmas Eve. I have often wondered whether this denial – and the consequent yearning – has given me special delight in getting a tree in adult life.

Each year I consider the practicality of a fake tree, and each year my children are so shocked by the suggestion that we end up with a real one. Getting it home and into its holder is always a fraught activity. But then comes the sigh of relief and anticipation. A huge bare tree awaits decoration.

As with everything to do with Christmas, an absolute tradition has to be followed here. Fascinating, isn't it, how important this seems to be at Christmas and how it sticks for life? This can lead to differences of opinion when different family traditions collide. I'm glad to say in our house mine has won!

There is never any question of going for a one-colour or minimalist look. Everything bar the kitchen sink has to go on the tree and the whole family helps. There are angels made in primary school cheek by jowl with battered Santas and spanking new jewel-encrusted baubles. When the lights are added (coloured seem fashionable at the moment, though I was brought up with the idea only white were 'good taste'), the whole thing is wildly over the top.

I love watching it in the evenings, with all the lights twinkling, because it means Christmas has truly begun!

Babies

Babies are wonderful.

They have an amazing effect on us all, connecting us to the future.

When you are pregnant there is a strange phenomenon no one warns you about: complete strangers start talking to you about your pregnancy and the occasional person actually asks to touch your bump. I found this disconcerting until I realized it's because babies somehow belong to everyone. We have a common investment in them as the future generation. Once you see that, it's actually rather touching.

Babies are also very funny in the way they laugh at strangers and soften even the most pompous personality. As long as they are fed and watered and changed, they are also incredibly happy, with a tough, wilful strength of their own.

I took a photograph of one of my daughters at six

months and am amazed each time I look at it. There she is, laughing, a small baby, yet the spark in her eye is absolutely the same then as she has now at 18. At six months she was somehow already a compete person.

Air Conditioning

Coming as I do from a cool country, I find air conditioning is still something new – and miraculous!

Keeping cool literally does keep you cool mentally as well as physically. It also means you can sleep, no matter how hot the night.

Car journeys are transformed. Traffic jams become bearable. Road rage is probably wildly reduced. Whenever I drive I put the air con on max, which annoys my children beyond measure. I, on the other hand, adore it. I can bowl along with my hair blowing in the cold breeze and arrive looking and feeling cool, calm and collected.

The first time I encountered air conditioning in cars was many years ago in the US. We noticed water pouring out from under the engine and took the car back to the rental agency to complain.

'Why is all that water pouring out?' I demanded crossly.

'Ma'am,' the clerk looked at me in amazement, 'that's the run-off from the air conditioning.'

Writing Postcards

I love postcards.

I love the whole ritual of looking for that one perfect card that captures the beauty, mood and soul of the place you're staying in, from Bognor to the Bahamas.

And then, what to write? Whether to be informative, witty, truthful or envy-inducing?

I know postcards do have some similarities with the gruesome round robin, where no bad news is allowed in. Smelly drains, overbooked hotels, crowded airports and food poisoning are laid aside amid lyrical descriptions of sunlit balconies, breathtaking vistas, crystal water and crimson sunsets.

On the practical front, we took someone else's teenager on holiday with us one year and her mother had included a roll of ready-addressed labels for her to stick on her postcards. It was the perfect way of remembering all those diabolical post codes. Each year I mean to do the same but always forget. So I end up guessing my friends' addresses. Perhaps they never receive the cards. And maybe it doesn't matter.

The whole point of postcards, it seems to me, is the act of writing them. Whether they arrive or not!

Rediscovering Something in Your Wardrobe

Buying something new is always a pleasure, but sometimes an even greater pleasure is the transforming effect the new thing can have on the rest of the clothes in your wardrobe. You buy one simple T-shirt or jumper and suddenly two or three outfits come together. It's like magic!

I know lots of people consult colour counsellors or image gurus who take one look at your wardrobe and put this skirt with that jacket and hey, presto! You're Elle Macpherson!

I've always been either too proud, too mean or too busy to opt for that. But I do get a real kick when I achieve a little bit of it myself. It's like being given a whole set of new clothes – without spending more than the cost of one new jumper.

Mobile Phones

Aren't mobile phones amazing? How did we survive without being able to call up and say we're delayed/ track a late child/find out if the broccoli on the shopping list really has to be purple sprouting?

Sure, they're intrusive and don't you want to kill people on trains or in restaurants who have inane conversations on them in extra loud voices? But still…

And they're such good entertainment systems. The photos you can take. The films you can make. My son and his friend amuse themselves for hours making sports commentaries and blogs about their schooldays on mine.

One unexpected result of the development of mobile phones has been the rise of romantic assignations – and often not with current partners. Surveys have shown that sexy texts, mobile messages and even e-mails have led to a huge rise in marital infidelity. Some people, it's claimed, even buy a mobile just to speak to the person they're having an affair with!

But, all in all, I greatly enjoy mobile-mania. Human beings just *have* to communicate, especially the female of the species, and this is the best way, so far, to do it.

Shopping in Markets

Markets are wonderful places and in an ideal world I'd always shop in them. But the world isn't ideal and I end up doing 99 per cent of my shopping in supermarkets.

The plus side of this is that markets remain a treat, something to be indulged in when you have a little longer and don't need to get everything from toilet rolls to pork chops to birthday cards in the same place.

French markets always seem especially gorgeous. The patience and the passion, the knowledge and the enthusiasm of the stallholders are treats in themselves.

But leather markets in Italy, flea markets in Paris, farmers' markets in the US and the fakes markets in Shanghai are all fabulous places to browse and shop. Even car boot sales have some of the marketplace about them. I suppose it's the personal relationship you get when buying on such a small scale that is great. Not to mention all that fantastic sales patter. Markets turn even the most mundane shopping into a lovely leisure pursuit.

And as well as buying the product, you feel you're buying a little of its history. Last year I bought fresh vegetables 'just grown' by a blue-bereted farmer in a small market in southwest France. When I examined them I found they were not that fresh – somewhat worm-eaten and infested with tiny spiders in fact. I had to laugh at myself. I realized I'd been buying *the idea* of the produce grown by a smallholder in *la France profonde*. Supermarkets would never have sold such shoddy goods. But they couldn't have given me half of the fun I had in making the purchase.

Kinky Boots

There is something universally wonderful about boots. They can be sexy, military or Boho, depending on the cut and what they're made of, but they are an instant outfit-transformer.

At 16 I bought a pair of white cut-out boots made by Courrèges, the must-have of the moment; at 21 I had a red knee-length pair. These were followed by damson suede boots by Biba, followed by countless others in leather, fabric and even (oh God) silver vinyl.

In fact, now that I think of it, we could probably all trace our lives in footwear! But I know one thing: killer stilettos may look vampish, but for a combination of style and comfort there's nothing to beat boots!

Spring

Every season has its wonders – the glowing russets and mellow yellows of autumn, with its mists and dew sparkling on spiders' webs; the frosty quietness and clear bright light of winter; the hot lazy days of summer, with evenings that seem to go on forever – but there is nothing like spring.

Spring brings the promise of renewal, regrowth, the belief that it's possible to start all over again no matter how dead life seems. It has touched the human soul from the beginning of time. Once people might have hummed, 'Summer is a-comin' in, loudly sing cuckoo,' now we just head for pavement cafés or the great outdoors. But spring is not just about the arrival of sunshine. It is a metaphor, perhaps the most profound of all metaphors, for hope, optimism and the sense that no matter how hard life is, there are better days ahead.

One of my favourite images of hope is the sight of a clump of snowdrops penetrating the pristine whiteness of a snowfall.

And one of the most spirit-lifting moments of the year comes when suddenly, often out of nowhere, the air warms up and you feel an irresistible urge to get outside.

Then you know spring has finally arrived.

Avoiding Mirrors

The singer Jarvis Cocker was once asked to give a piece of advice on life. His answer was: 'Avoid looking at yourself in mirrors in lifts.'

He was trying to be funny, obviously, but I feel there is a grain of truth here and I extend it to all mirrors.

The way I interpret this is not to get too obsessed with how you look, because most people don't really study you and it just makes you feel bad!

Over the years I've noticed that if I spend ages getting ready for a party or important work occasion, the longer I spend, the worse I feel. So I have evolved the ultimate confidence-boosting Getting Ready to Go Out system. I work out what I'm going to wear, right down to tights and jewellery, and hang it up on a hanger. Then I whizz in and change into it in record time, looking in the mirror for just one brief second to make sure my skirt isn't stuck in my tights.

It's amazing how much more attractive and positive this makes me feel.

Thank you, Jarvis Cocker.

Reading Catalogues

There is something wonderful about catalogues. Catalogues for clothing. Catalogues for homeware. Even catalogues for ludicrous garden ornaments when you happen to live on the eighth floor with no balcony.

First there's the fun of wondering why they were sent to you in the first place. What made some company imagine you were yearning for long-sleeved silk underwear or professional chef's kitchen knives or plus-sized nightdresses?

Most of them, I have to admit, go straight in the bin, but there are a select few I keep for pleasurable browsing.

An old lady of my acquaintance keeps seed catalogues by the side of her bed, hidden from her husband as an adolescent boy might keep *Penthouse* hidden from his mum. Her husband says she already spends far too much money on seeds. She says looking is free.

And that's the attraction. Part of the appeal of catalogues

is that you can fantasize about owning something without spending a penny. And the best-designed ones are a pleasure to read – like a glossy magazine without the cover price.

And now and then you have the even greater delight of finding something that really is right for you – and buying it.

Using the Five Minutes

At the convent boarding school where I was educated the nuns had a really wise and helpful saying: 'Use the five minutes.' By this they often meant you should use them to say a quick prayer or do something good, but I have adapted this to modern life, where I interpret it as: 'Get on with something while you are sitting at a traffic light, waiting for the washing machine to finish or on the tube travelling to a meeting.'

I'm not sure why I find multi-tasking such a huge pleasure. I think it's because I can't bear wasted time and always like to be getting on with something. My mother, a full-time doctor and mother of four who hated housework, used to point out how much cleaning could be done in five minutes with a Kleenex tissue. I'm just the same.

Maybe the reward comes in feeling you're yanking back a few precious moments from the hamster-wheel of life. I don't know whether this is a modern phenomenon or if cave-woman got a kick from brushing out the ashes while simultaneously skinning a mastodon, but it seems to be an especially female pleasure. Men like to focus on one thing at a time. That's too boring for women, who want to get it all over with so that they can put their feet up and chat on the phone while sipping a coffee at the same time.

I was once sent a fabulous birthday card entitled 'He Makes the Tea/She Makes the Tea' which really got it spot on. In the 'He' version the man leans on the Aga whistling, waiting for the kettle to boil. In the 'She' version, in exactly the same time, she puts on the washing, lets the dog out, takes out the rubbish and empties the dishwasher!

In London, where I live, the authorities are always trying to ban that hate-figure 'the school-run mum' who is guilty of taking up valuable road space while 'simply' dropping kids off at school. The mums had a great reply. They didn't 'simply' drop off their kids. They did a shop, took the cat to the vet, bought stamps, filled up on petrol and delivered stuff to the charity shop, often on their way to full-time or part-time jobs. I'd like to see a man achieve as much in so little time – and all without making any fuss about it!

Stainless-steel Saucepans

About 15 years ago my husband spent an enormous sum on stainless-steel saucepans. They came in a set with about 100 different bits. I fumed and put it down to male extravagance. I had seen the ads for this set of 'Professional Cook's' wildly expensive saucepans and thought, 'Who on earth would buy those?'

My husband would.

But I was wrong. Unlike all the non-stick pans that have come and gone in our kitchen, those pans have lasted all that time without a scratch.

And the joy of cleaning them! You can use the toughest, meanest scouring tools and they come out sparkling every time.

I think if I was going to give one boring-but-useful gift to make my daughters' and son's lives easier when they set up home it would be a set of stainless-steel Professional Cook's saucepans. And hang the cost!

Giving to Charity Shops

It's the perfect design idea. Most of us in the Western world own too much. Shopping tends to be a hobby rather than a necessity and women's magazines are always estimating that we only wear 20 per cent of the clothes we buy anyway.

Enter the charity shop.

Prompted by a house move or a season change, we decide to chuck away all that stuff we don't really need. All six bin-bags of it.

And still our wardrobes are full, because throwing stuff out isn't easy. A voice inside your head stops you. 'Hey, hang on,' it says, 'that might come in handy if you're asked to a Venetian masked ball/distant relative's funeral/alpine ski lodge/St Petersburg.'

Giving to a charity shop, knowing that the clothes will be genuinely useful to someone else, can get you over this blockage.

I have to admit I'm a terrible hoarder and so never want to throw anything out, so I have developed a clever technique: 'Put it in the bin-liner and then we'll keep it for six months.' This acts as a kind of security blanket. If I haven't needed it in six months then it can safely go to the charity shop.

Then, of course, I may suddenly decide I want it after all. But by now, as I remind myself, it's enjoying a new life with someone else. And Cancer Research, Christian Aid or the hospice movement is surely more important than a frilly top. Isn't it?

Seizing the Day

I had to go for a routine mammogram not long ago and I put a list on my door entitled: 'What I Would Do If I Had a Bad Mammogram'.

One of my daughters told me I was weird and said, 'Why don't you just do these things anyway?'

It was a good question. Why do we need a horrible jolt to tell us we should get on with doing the things we want to do in life?

Maybe because we're too busy, or they seem selfish, or we're actually scared of doing some of the things we think we want to do.

One of my friends had as her New Year's resolution: 'Have more fun generally.'

Like the list on my door, it's surprisingly hard to make yourself have more fun.

But I'm certainly going to try.

Being Creative

Creativity comes in so many forms. We tend to see it as something big and grand like painting a masterpiece or writing a great novel, but actually it is anything you do that gives you artistic satisfaction.

I know lots of very high-powered women who love nothing better than stitching a bit of embroidery, and one of my most successful friends, a Cambridge professor, once asked me to go on a flower-arranging course with her! I don't really know why I was surprised, since I know how wonderfully diverse women are in their interests and satisfactions. And I believe an outlet for our creative urges is vital, and very enjoyable too.

Last Christmas I made my own wreath for the front door and really enjoyed feeling I was resisting the overwhelming tide of commercialism. The high point of October for me used to be decorating harvest festival baskets for my kids to take to school – though they later confessed they were embarrassed being seen with them when other mums sent in two tins of beans in a Tesco bag! One of my daughters paints beautifully and makes amazing place settings; the other ices cakes for her schoolmates. The last cake had a hammer and sickle iced on it to mark studying Communism in their history class!

Creativity can come in so many forms, from choosing the perfect colour for your kitchen to putting roses in a vase to laying a lovely Christmas table. In the end, it's about making things personal and putting your own particular stamp on the objects around you so that you smile every time you look at them.

Having Daughters

Perhaps a large rather than a small pleasure, this.

Sometimes mothers and daughters say they are best friends, which makes me sceptical, especially as some of the biggest rows I've had in my life have been with my daughters. My daughters aren't my best friends, nor I theirs, but they are an enormous source of delight and pleasure.

When daughters are small there is the fun of dressing them (though not in the same outfits – I once got into terrible trouble for doing this). And then there's the pleasure of watching them grow into the people they will one day be.

With my own daughters I'm now at a point of transition. Until now I have been very much the adult, the one in charge – at least nominally! Now they are becoming grown women, our relationship is changing.

There is a wonderful song called 'Turn Around' by

Malvina Reynolds that sums up how quickly this all seems to take place, even though it's actually over many years. One moment your daughter is a little girl in 'sunsuits and petticoats', and the next time you turn around, she's a teenager on her first date, and when you turn around again she's a young wife with babies of her own.

I haven't reached that stage yet, but I do realize how precious and special this mother–daughter relationship is. There have been times when we've wanted to kill each other, but in the end I couldn't be more grateful that my daughters came along.

An Early Night

When I was a child, being sent to bed early was a terrible punishment. Now, in one of those funny twists of fate, I find it a great pleasure.

There is something wonderfully comforting about making yourself a hot drink, selecting an exciting novel, an unread magazine or a favourite TV show and disappearing up to bed.

This is an even greater treat in winter, when you can cosy up under the duvet with the happy thought that it's dark outside and morning won't be arriving for a long time yet.

Sometimes it's fun to share your early night with a partner, but the best and purest pleasure, in my opinion anyway, is to enjoy it on your own!

Running after a Bus and Actually Catching It!

There is a very funny sketch by the American comic Bob Newhart where bus drivers are at an instructor's school which teaches them to sail right past anyone who tries to flag them down.

Like all the best comedy, it's drawn from life. We all know that feeling when we run for a bus and just as we get near the stop it drives off, leaving us wondering if the driver did it purposely.

But just now and then we catch the bus. And what a wonderful feeling it is! The risk of almost missing it doubles our pleasure in actually managing to get on.

It's like the euphoria you feel when you almost miss a train or plane but just make it in the nick of time. Instead of experiencing a boring or run-of-the-mill journey, you feel as though you've been given a present!

Picking Mushrooms

There is nothing to rival the taste of absolutely fresh mushrooms which you have picked yourself, washed and cooked in butter and piled onto toast within half an hour of finding them.

Any 'food for free' is satisfying. I love blackberrying, scrumping for apples and hunting for wild strawberries, but picking mushrooms is the best of all.

The hunt is part of the pleasure. Mushrooms start to appear in early autumn and are best picked in the early morning. There are hundreds of varieties in my mushroom guide, but the most dramatic I've ever seen is the puffball – literally as big as a football, often perfectly spherical, and virtually white in colour. It doesn't look as if it could possibly be edible and yet it is delicious – fragrant and woody tasting. I have a much-prized photo of my two daughters holding one when they were eight and ten and can still remember how great it tasted when we shared it with our neighbour after the photo was taken.

Field mushrooms are becoming very fashionable. They are sold for a lot of money and feature on the menu in smart restaurants. But there's nothing quite like the joy of finding your own.

They lurk together in clumps and according to country lore the best are found where there is both horse and cow dung in the same field – a fact I prefer not to dwell on when I am tucking into a delicious plateful of them!

Almost Giving Up on a Job Then Finding You Can Do It

I have to confess that when it comes to home improvement I come from the Homer Simpson school of 'If a job's hard, then it isn't worth doing'. Screws stick in the rawlplug, nails bend and holes appear in the wall whenever I attempt DIY. But the element of almost giving up and resisting it does make finishing a job so satisfying. And it avoids the feeling of defeat you get when you give a task up halfway through.

The actual occurrence that promoted this realization was the fixing on of a new toilet seat which appeared to have metal attachments designed for a completely different model. This led to much swearing and the accusation that it was all my fault for purchasing inferior sanitary ware.

And then, finally, the right screws went in and *voila*! a

brand new loo seat and the satisfaction of not having given up halfway!

Being Grumpy

I know pleasure is supposed to be about sweetness and light and embracing all humanity etc. etc., but there are darker satisfactions; and being grumpy is one of them.

Sometimes, to hell with it, you're in a bad mood and you feel like showing it. So you snap at people. You shoot out black looks like Milton's Lucifer. You are picky. You moan. You take pleasure in the misfortunes of others. You don't 'move on', as the clichéd advice would have you do. You stay right where you are: angry.

And then, just as suddenly, you feel better.

Pitta Bread

When I was a child, pitta bread was unknown. Now it's a delicious and essential addition to our everyday diets. Like pizza, bagels, pesto, croissants or garlic bread, it is an exotic import that we have so taken to our hearts that we hardly remember it's foreign.

Part of the wonder of pitta lies in the fact it is a pocket and can therefore be stuffed with more or less anything you like. The other fabulous attribute is how quick it is to toast or grill. It is delicious and versatile. You can heat it in the oven and dip it in hummus or taramasalata, or stuff it with lamb souvlaki and shredded cabbage like they do in Greece and Turkey. One of the greatest of student pleasures is to eat pitta in the street stuffed with doner kebab till the grease runs down your fingers.

With the right filling, it can even be good for you!

Fresh Snow

Is the world ever lovelier or more awe-inspiring than after a snowfall? There is something about the grey-yellow quality of the light, the stillness and the silence that really does turn the mind towards the divine.

Snow is also wonderful fun: skiing, snowboarding and tobogganing all fill you with exhilaration and the sense of being incredibly alive. Just like the little boy in *The Snowman*, we can't wait to rush out into it, to be the very first to imprint our footsteps onto that blank white canvas.

I had to take one of my daughters for hospital tests once and when we came out the whole city was buried under a snowfall. 'Do I *have* to go to school?' she asked. For once in my life I came up with the right answer. We bought a silly throwaway camera and went to Hampstead Heath, a huge wild space full of lakes and trees, and spent the next two hours gambolling in the snow and taking silly pictures that I still treasure.

As the climate warms up, snow is getting rarer and rarer – in this country at least – and a snowfall, in my opinion, gives you instant permission to spend as long as you want in it. And no one is allowed to call you to account for it!

Going to Sleep

No matter how tired you are, your brain sometimes snaps awake just at the wrong moment.

I have always been a bit of an insomniac, which (flatteringly!) I attribute to being exceptionally energetic. My mother was the same. Despite being a full-time doctor and the mother of four, if she couldn't sleep she would get up in the middle of the night and start painting ceilings.

Which is all very well, but it does leave you exhausted in the morning. So I have tried many techniques to get myself to sleep in the dark watches of the night. This is the only one that really seems to work. Get yourself into the position that you most often sleep in and then go back in time to a house you once lived in. I take myself back to the home we once had on the seafront of a small provincial town. I start outside in the street and walk down the garden path and through the front door. From there I walk through each room, trying to recall every picture, colour scheme and piece of furniture in as much detail as possible. I find I rarely get beyond the ground floor before I fall asleep.

It doesn't have to be a house – it can be any memory that you can recall in exact detail. It's the detail that does it, by distracting you from the swirling thoughts that are rushing round your brain and keeping you awake.

Psychologists apparently have a proper name for this – visualization – but it doesn't need a name. It just works!

Not Bearing Grudges

There are all sorts of reasons to bear grudges: spouses who leave you, bosses who ignore you, family members who take you for granted. And yet the truism that bearing grudges only hurts you is actually true!

One of the other pleasures I've listed here is allowing yourself to wallow in self-pity and I absolutely endorse that, but when you've wallowed your fill, then it's time to (in that ghastly phrase) 'move on'.

Relationships are wrecked, friendships sabotaged and family rifts deepened by holding on to a grudge.

Let it go.

You'll feel better afterwards.

Going to the Hairdresser's

Hairdressers are special.

They know us inside out. They know that when it comes to a haircut we want 'just a little off' and that we will rarely, if ever, wildly change our hair colour.

They also know whether we're generous or mean, exuberant or shy. And they know an awful lot about our personal lives.

Recently there was an outcry here when a firm of divorce lawyers started paying hairdressers to inform them of impending marriage splits. People were outraged! Hairdressers are like confessors. Part of the pleasure of visiting them is to moan about our husbands or lovers in the strictest confidence.

Visiting my own hairdresser's is always great fun. Men are of course admitted these days, but they rarely dare cross the threshold, and if they do, they scuttle away as soon as possible.

Spas have never been as much fun. There is something solitary about spa treatments, no matter how indulgent they are. Give me the jokey camaraderie of the hairdresser's over the anonymous exclusiveness of the spa any day!

Family Meals

OK, in this rushing, swirling pressured world, this may be more of an aspiration than an everyday reality. It's very hard to gather everyone together round one table, but there is a lot of evidence that the family that eats together stays together. Or at least has a greater chance of doing so.

Perhaps one of the reasons for this is that sharing a family meal gives everyone the chance to contribute – through the cooking, table-laying and clearing-up – and that can bring everyone together, even if they are a bit unwilling.

Conversations can get heated, of course, especially if this isn't something you do every day, but usually with the whole family present things get resolved, if only by someone saying, 'Just say sorry, then we can all watch TV.'

In England there's a rather scary statistic that a third of families no longer possess a table to eat at, which

– if true – is really sad. I do think a table is a bit of a metaphor for how family life works. It's no accident that negotiators talk about 'getting round a table' as a way of sorting problems out.

Europeans often say that the way to teach young people to drink responsibly is at family meals, though in our house I fear it would teach them how to drink 'irresponsibly'!

Watching Your Children Sleep

I'm not sure why this is so pleasurable, but it is. And it doesn't matter how old the children are – toddlers or teenagers, or even adults.

Maybe it's because it reminds you of the few moments of peace you had when they were tiny. Or perhaps it's because sleeping faces are so innocent, so childlike, and fill you with protective and silent love.

Even if the children are difficult and bolshie when awake, in sleep their faces are as tender and hopeful as new buds on an apple tree in Maytime.

Irresistible.

Pottering in the Garden

It used to be said that you were closest to God in a garden. Whether you find that convincing or not, there's something incredibly soothing about gardening.

Sometimes it's the physical exercise involved in digging or clearing that makes you feel better. And gardening is full of weeding and planting and deadheading, all of which seem to have great metaphoric significance for the human spirit.

Added to that there's the simple pleasure of being outdoors, feeling the sun on your back and seeing the garden wildlife all around you. I counted no fewer than four frogs this year in our tiny garden pond and although I don't like frogs much (unlike our cat, who watched them for hours, still as the cat in Mr MacGregor's garden), it was still rather amazing that they'd chosen to live there.

And lastly, even if you're a pretty amateur gardener like me, there's the powerful pleasure of creating a space that is beautiful to look at and delightful to sit in.

In fact I can think of few activities that offer you so many rewards on so many different levels. But then, as everyone knows, we Brits are just nutty about our gardens!

Birds on a Bird Table

A bird table is a joy. For the price of a few peanuts, all sorts of species come right up to your window.

As long as you put the nuts out in a special feeder (otherwise the hated squirrels get them; squirrels are very smart, the Doctor Nos of the garden world), a whole range of birds will come and perform for you, creating your very own wildlife programme. This year we had jays, blue tits, blackbirds and even a green woodpecker visiting regularly.

The woodpecker positioned himself upside down and snacked for hours on our nuts. I could hear him laughing as he flew off (woodpeckers usually call in flight). Although he didn't sound anything like the famous Woody, it was still a privilege to have him visit.

Finding Something Is Cheaper than You Thought

It's always an unexpected pleasure when you go to pay for something and find the price has been slashed.

This happened to me the other day when buying a new dress. I went to pay and, inexplicably, the price came up a third less than on the ticket. Then, of course, I went through the temporary agony of wondering whether it was a mistake and, if so, should I point it out?

In this case I didn't mention it. I decided luck was on my side. And I went around feeling really good for hours!

A Cool Pillow

This is one my 13-year-old son suggested and I absolutely agree with him.

There is nothing as soothing as putting your face against the inviting smooth freshness of a cool clean pillow.

For Mother's Day last year one of my daughters gave me a spray called 'Perfect Sleep Pillow Mist', which made me (secretly) roar with laughter at the absurdity of a society that could produce such a thing. But actually … it's really pleasant, leaving the pillow smelling of mandarin, chamomile and lavender. And it really does smell of them, being made of pure flower extracts rather than chemicals. Of course it's a bit silly, but the awful confession is I've become rather addicted to it – and I think it really does help you sleep too!

Holding a Small Child's Hand

When a small child slips their hand into yours, you feel an amazing sense of wellbeing.

I suppose it's down to the feeling of trust.

Perhaps it's the fact that you're the grown-up, no matter how un-grown-up you may feel.

Perhaps it's just that there is something physical and delightful about fitting a small hand into the protectiveness of a larger one.

Or maybe it's the sudden connection between yourself and future generations.

Whatever the explanation, holding a small child's hand is a powerful pleasure. The interesting thing is that though we may feel this most strongly with our own children or grandchildren, we also feel moved by holding the hand of any child.

We may look with a certain cynicism at celebrities cuddling African children, but the trusting innocence of very young children does make us question what we're doing about the future. So maybe, for once, we should give the celebs the benefit of the doubt.

Changing a Fuse

Whenever a friend phones to say how depressed they're feeling about their job/marriage/kids (and we all feel this way sometimes), I always recommend they do a small, simple task.

When you can't change the big things, doing something small and routine that you are guaranteed to succeed at does wonders for your sense of self.

In this category I would include: tidying the airing cupboard (a neat row of towels always cheers), deadheading flowers, tidying your office and – best of all – changing a fuse.

Obviously you can't go round changing fuses that don't need it, but if one does need it, this small task is like a miracle. You feel instantly competent, together, in charge, no matter how much panic is lapping at your feet.

Doing something small and practical is the micromanaging equivalent of taking one day at a time.

Wearing Cashmere

Cashmere used to be the provenance of the very rich. Even the name evokes luxury and exclusiveness, *après-ski* for expensive blondes in Aspen or St Moritz. There is even a fragrance that uses the name to evoke a promise of being pricily pampered. But now cashmere has wildly dropped in cost and, with a bit of saving, most of us can afford a cashmere sweater or scarf.

And there's nothing quite like the feeling of cashmere next to the skin. It is unique – softer than lamb's wool and not as itchy as angora. No wonder, at least in fantasy, that cashmere is matched with that other gloriously glamorous fabric, silk.

Most glam of all is the cashmere sweater in winter-white, a garment that never fails to look expensive and luxurious – even if it actually comes from Marks and Spencer!

Walking Barefoot Where the Sand Meets the Sea

Walking barefoot is lovely anyway – feeling the sand between your toes always sums up summer for me – but walking along the line of the sand and the sea is loveliest of all.

Holidays tend to be about lying on sunbeds feeling hedonistic, but the one activity you always have energy for is a stroll along the water's edge, in a bikini or with your skirt hitched up, sandals in your hand, perhaps even as the sun goes down on the distant horizon.

Memories, as they say, are made of this.

A Really Good Haircut

Men are always marvelling at how much women spend on their hair. How can a woman need to have hers done every single month?

The answer is that she is always hoping for a really good haircut, the kind that transforms you from average to stunning.

This is a holy grail she will pursue her whole life long, despite all the disillusions and disasters, through hideous curly perms that leave her looking like Harpo Marx, hair straightenings that evoke Morticia Addams and mistaken attempts to emulate Jennifer Aniston.

Each time she will take a photo clipped from a magazine and eagerly hand it over. Rarely or ever will she learn.

But, no matter. Once every five years she will end up with a Really Good Haircut. And that will keep her going through the next five.

Creating New Habits

I read somewhere that you only have to do a thing three times for it to start becoming a habit. Unfortunately this applies to bad as well as good habits.

But a new habit can soon become a new pleasure.

Recently I found myself talked into dropping my daughter at her inconveniently distant school once a week. When the traffic is bad it can take hours to get there and at first I'd get quite grumpy, wishing I'd never agreed to it. But then I began to enjoy some revealing conversations with my daughter on the way there. And I discovered that the supermarket near the school baked cantuccini which were not only chocolate flavoured but also dipped in Belgian chocolate. They were seriously the most delicious treat I had ever tasted. So soon this irritating journey brought not only a sense of intimacy with my daughter but also the reward of a latte plus chocolate cantuccini!

In fact, I have to confess, I looked forward to both with

equal pleasure and was quite sad when my daughter finally left that school.

Champagne

Let's get one thing straight: I love anything with bubbles – Cava from Spain, Prosecco from Venice, vin Mousseux from the southwest of France, fizzy Chardonnay from New Zealand and Australia. But none of them, no matter how good, comes anywhere near champagne.

Wine writers often say a good fizz rivals a bad champagne. Be that as it may, nothing, but nothing, comes near a good champagne.

I used to have a boss who said a glass of good champagne at noon made you happy for the rest of the day, and if I'm ever rich enough to carry it through – or employ anyone other than myself – I might emulate him and say, 'Champagne, everyone!' instead of seeing what they want for elevenses.

There is a certain amount of self-discipline involved in having just the one glass, but I think that given the very best champagne, I might be able to manage it.

Crazy Christmas Lights

I love the trend, new in this country, of neighbours trying to outdo each other with crazy Christmas lights.

All over the land, rooftop nativity scenes are suddenly vying with flashing snowmen and eight-foot blow-up Santas, not to mention Rudolf, Dasher, Dancer *et al.*, life-size, picked out in multi-coloured fairy lights. Half the suburban semis are now trying to rival Harrod's or Macy's with their Christmas illuminations.

Some people argue that they're vulgar and tasteless and ought to be banned, but I love them.

A homeowner not too far from us in north London lights up the whole of his house with every possible combination of sleigh, Father Christmas, Baby Jesus, angel and reindeer. This year he added a walk-in Santa's grotto. I suspect one of these Yuletides a busy official will put the lid on it, but for now it's become an unofficial attraction. And every time I drive past, it makes me smile.

And last but not least…

Froth on the Cappuccino

Can there be anything more delicious than sprinkling fresh chocolate onto your cappuccino and eating the froth, slowly and sensuously, as befits its amazing wondrousness?

I feel sorry for sad and sophisticated espresso drinkers. Think what they're missing! And herbal tea may be excellent for the digestion, but it's hardly mouth-wateringly delicious.

And what about the joy of the takeaway cappuccino with that last inch of foam lurking at the bottom of the paper cup?

Mmmmmm … heaven!

Titles of Related Interest

Notes For Your Own Pleasures

Notes For Your Own Pleasure

Notes For Your Own Pleasures

HAY HOUSE PUBLISHERS

We hope you enjoyed this Hay House book.
If you would like to receive a free catalogue featuring additional
Hay House books and products, or if you would like information
about the Hay Foundation, please contact:

Hay House UK Ltd
292B Kensal Rd • London W10 5BE
Tel: (44) 20 8962 1230; Fax: (44) 20 8962 1239
www.hayhouse.co.uk

***

Published and distributed in the United States of America by:
Hay House, Inc. • PO Box 5100 • Carlsbad, CA 92018-5100
Tel.: (1) 760 431 7695 or (1) 800 654 5126;
Fax: (1) 760 431 6948 or (1) 800 650 5115
www.hayhouse.com

Published and distributed in Australia by:
Hay House Australia Ltd • 18/36 Ralph St • Alexandria NSW 2015
Tel.: (61) 2 9669 4299; Fax: (61) 2 9669 4144
www.hayhouse.com.au

Published and distributed in the Republic of South Africa by:
Hay House SA (Pty) Ltd • PO Box 990 • Witkoppen 2068
Tel./Fax: (27) 11 467 8904 • www.hayhouse.co.za

Published and distributed in India by:
Hay House Publishers India • Muskaan Complex • Plot No.3
B-2 • Vasant Kunj • New Delhi – 110 070.
Tel.: (91) 11 41761620; Fax: (91) 11 41761630.
www.hayhouse.co.in

Distributed in Canada by:
Raincoast • 9050 Shaughnessy St • Vancouver, BC V6P 6E5
Tel.: (1) 604 323 7100; Fax: (1) 604 323 2600

***

Sign up via the Hay House UK website to receive the Hay House
online newsletter and stay informed about what's going on with
your favourite authors. You'll receive bimonthly announcements
about discounts and offers, special events, product highlights,
free excerpts, giveaways, and more!
www.hayhouse.co.uk